MOTHERS

and

LEADERSHIP

MOTHERS
and
LEADERSHIP

Twelve Principles for Success

HOW STUDYING THE LEADERSHIP PRINCIPLES,
EXAMPLES AND STYLES OF MOTHERS WILL MAKE
YOU A BETTER LEADER AND PERSON TODAY

Motivation Optimism Momentum (MOM)

Reginald E. Vance, Ph.D.

IN COLLABORATION WITH PHENOMENAL AUTHORS AND CONTRIBUTORS

Archway Publishing books may be ordered through booksellers or by contacting:

Archway Publishing
1663 Liberty Drive
Bloomington, IN 47403
www.archwaypublishing.com
844-669-3957

Unless otherwise noted, scripture quotations taken from The Holy Bible, New International Version® NIV® Copyright © 1973 1978 1984 2011 by Biblica, Inc. TM Used by permission. All rights reserved worldwide.

Scripture marked (KJV) taken from the King James Version of the Bible.

ISBN: 978-1-6657-2354-1 (sc)
ISBN: 978-1-6657-2443-2 (hc)
ISBN: 978-1-6657-2355-8 (e)

Library of Congress Control Number: 2022908474

Print information available on the last page.

Archway Publishing rev. date: 6/3/2022

CONTENTS

DEDICATION

This book is dedicated to my Mother and all the
mothers who have made and are making a leadership
difference in the lives of those who dare to lead.

Amelia Julia Vance is affectionately known as "Momma V" by so many
people I grew up with and she helped raise, as well as by the extended
family members, friends, co-workers, brothers, sisters, cousins, and fraternity Brothers she nurtured over the years. She and mothers like her is
who this compendium of leadership testimonies is all about. Our mothers lived and are living lives of leadership exemplified by the perilous
challenges they met, faced, and overcame without complaint. This book
is dedicated to their selfless, diligent lives and undying souls.

On January 20, 1938, Momma V was born Amelia Julia Thomas-
James in Brinkley, Arkansas. She was born on the heels of the Great

Depression. While in Arkansas, she graduated from high school despite the tremendous odds posed by a teenage marriage, bearing children at an early age while picking the King's cotton.

Mother overcame some of the most traumatic hardships one can imagine. Low wages with long work hours, limited experience, and stunted career opportunities based on race and gender inequalities were but a few obstacles which inspired her to strive for excellence and independence through her poised, nurturing leadership style. She accomplished so much with so little. Despite her limited resources, Momma V always found a way to help others. She helped so many.

The life of Momma V, as well as caring mothers around the globe, offers an untold story of authentic leadership that deserves universal attention, compassion, celebration, and sharing.

This book is dedicated to my mother, Amelia J. Vance. One of the greatest leaders the world will ever have the pleasure of knowing.

ACKNOWLEDGEMENTS

Primarily, I acknowledge God Almighty for Blessing me with a mother who cultivated my leadership desires, abilities, and successes. I also acknowledge His goodness, grace, and mercy for blessing me with other mother-like figures, wonderful friends and dedicated family members who believe in me. Ms. Amelia J. Vance is the angel in life everyone hopes to have. I was blessed to have her as my mother, mentor and best friend for nearly 44 years. Even as she battled Stage 4 cancer at age 71, my mother remained a source of support and motivation, optimism and momentum. Posthumously, Momma V is a major contributor to this book project.

Mom, keep showing us how it's done.

I acknowledge all my brothers and sisters for the lessons they taught me during childhood and the lessons they continue to offer me in adulthood. Antoine, Michael, Sheila (rest in peace prior to my birth), Debra, Curtis, Loretha, Coletha, Aaron Jr. (rest in peace), Darlene, and Dorothy (rest in peace). I thank each of you for your leadership examples. I acknowledge my nephew Gerald Copeland and my niece Shaliss Vance (Simmons) who are the equivalent of the 12th and 13th children of the Amelia J. Vance clan.

I acknowledge the Brothers of Omega Psi Phi Fraternity, Incorporated for their eleven decades of community service and uplift to mankind. The principles and examples of leadership you embrace and exemplify make it easier for me to continue striving to help others with an URGENT sense of NOW and dedicated commitment to EXCELLENCE.

After contributing to numerous books, articles, reviews, and technical reports, I am embarking on my first independent book project with the help of true friends and family. This has been my dream for quite some time. This project could not have been accomplished without the support and contributions of others. I acknowledge all the authors and contributors near and dear as my consistent and continuous support system. Their unbridled encouragement provides the strength, guidance and stability required to pursue such an enormous undertaking. I owe a great debt of gratitude to those who helped and continue to help turn dreams into reality. Thank you Tyrza Cole (Reese) for helping to push us over the finish line.

I acknowledge all the contributors (Reverend Marcus Hillie, Reverend Doctor Dwain Harrell, Doctor Kwamme Anderson, Mayor Cashenna Cross, Bill Minix, Doctor Ira Credle, Reverend Ademuyiwa T. Bamiduro, Donald McKeever, Angelo Riddick, Danny Coleman, Christopher Pirtle, Cherron Jones, Reverend Dr. George Holmes, Christopher Simpson, Dr. James Anderson, Alisa Cowan, Sherman Charles, Taft Gaddy, Brett Smith and Jeannie Miles-Essone) as well as the many people who are mentioned in the stories shared throughout this book. We gratefully acknowledge all the mothers and mother-like figures who helped and continue to help shape our leadership styles and profiles. Many mothers are mentioned in this book and so many more are not due to the page constraints of this project. We acknowledge those not mentioned. We know who they are. We celebrate them in life. We acknowledge the mothers who are angels on high for persistently guiding our leadership journey.

FOREWORD

JOE LEONARD, JR. PH.D.

When Dr. Vance humbly asked me to write the forward to this soon to be staple in leadership studies, I was immediately honored and duty-bound to help a friend. His plight and experiences are indeed similar to my upbringing. We both share a profound love and compassion for the mothers who raised us. Also, we share a thirst to help others through our community service, civic engagements, and academic commitments.

So to recommend this book to leaders and future leaders in all facets of society is just one more worthy cause to improve the lives, careers, and education of those who share a genuine compassion to help others. That is what effective leadership demands, requires and denotes. Vance's fresh vision and unique perspective challenges me to recall a better book on the principles of effective leadership.

Mothers and Leadership is an excellent book that hearkens me back to my childhood in Austin, Texas, and my Grandparents residences in Mexia and Crockett Texas. The fundamental lessons I learned there are the lessons for success from a people that never gave up nor did they ever stop believing their children could prosper despite their segregated station. As I read the principles, I am reminded that ties are what bond one generation to another. More importantly, these jewels (principles) are what bond a generation that has suffered a great trauma to a generation that has lived in relative freedom. The younger generation will believe that freedom and the ability to realize dreams always existed, so it is up to older generations to pass down the principles of freedom and leadership just as the Hebrews of the Old Testament passed along the Bible to the world.

As I lost my mother eight years ago, I leave you with the words she would tell me as I went to school every morning, "Be good, smart, strong and wise make your family and ancestors proud and I will too".

This book is about the 12 P's, but it is also about the dignity of a people who sacrificed for future generations. We will never forget the "Momma V's" in all of our families.

With honor and reverence for our ancestors,
Joe Leonard, Jr., Ph.D.

PREFACE
MICHAEL ADAMS, ESQUIRE

Having recently lost my mother to a long battle with cancer, I understand the courage, strength, prayer, patience, preparation, and perseverance a family endures when caring for a mother who has been diagnosed with a terminal illness.

The leadership lessons in this book transcend not only academia and government service but can also be helpful tools in business development, personal growth and civic responsibility.

What Dr. Vance lays out in this book is a roadmap to successful techniques that can be used by anyone who aspires to be in the team leader role of a corporate 500 company, the chairperson of a local PTA, or the organizer of a family reunion.

I have been fortunate to have experienced seeing Dr. Vance excel and grow through his college experiences, professional challenges and personal developments. He is a new age thinker from the old school of hard knocks!

This work is a must read for those seeking an example of an inner-city black male who made it. He made it against the odds and has not forgotten the adage of helping to lift others as he climbs. More impressive is the fact that he made it while keeping the leadership lessons from his mother close to his heart and actions. It is rare to hear men broach the topic of their leadership capacity as it relates to their mothers' examples. It is even rarer for academicians, intellectuals, and writers to pen those experiences. Dr. Vance has gone far beyond the boundaries that restrain most leadership students, scholars, and practitioners.

The layout and design of this book are as impressive and thought provoking as the content of each Part and chapter. Vance brilliantly intertwines personal, family and work experiences together to unveil a splendid tapestry of life experiences that will cause people of all leadership walks to stop and think about how their mothers are truly the fabric of their lives.

From the inspirational poems by Momma V and her children to the heart-warming story sharing from the contributors of this uniquely crafted manuscript, each Part and chapter provides the reader with something to cling onto. If you are a leader or aspiring to be a leader, this book is for you.

Part One: Motivation provides the reader with four principles that all leaders I have known share in common-Prayer, Positivity, Patience and Praise. This Part is a tribute to those good things all people should possess, but effective leaders must possess.

Part Two: Optimism supplies the reader with four principles that successful organizations cannot survive without-Purpose, People, Persistence and Perspective. This Part is really about the steps and components required to form meaningful, hopeful and faithful relationships that are an integral part of effective leadership.

Part Three: Momentum introduces the leadership principles Priorities, Preparation, Perseverance, and Prosperity. Vance and the other contributors use this last Part to ignite the reader to be more attentive to the struggles and sacrifices that lend themselves to sustainable leadership. Once a leader grasps the final installment of effective leadership, they are ready to rocket toward success.

The twelve principals will surely provoke analysis in the way one provides the much-needed leadership and direction to civic, religious, and business leaders.

Every successful leader understands the importance of motivation. The power of prayer and the effects of praise. They understand optimism-keeping their purpose and people together.

And finally, they understand momentum. Timing is everything. Strike while the iron is hot!

This work will aid in gaining definition and understanding of effective leadership.

Michael R.D. Adams, Esq.

INTRODUCTION

"When time has recorded each of your actions and history has forever etched the final account of your deeds, what story will be told?"
Reginald E. Vance, Ph.D.

When I started this book project, my mother was still alive. The project started as a collection of poems my mother and I wrote to each other, family members, and friends. Much of that work is preserved and contained in this version. Throughout this book, you will meet several interesting people with authentic, exciting, interesting, organic, uplifting and sometimes painful leadership stories. The author and contributors provide ways, means and motives of why and how decisions are made at critical life and leadership junctures. So, let's begin.

On January 20, 2009, my Mother and I watched the swearing in of Barack Obama as the 44th president of the United States of America. We watched this inspiring event from the comforts of my home in Fort Washington, Maryland. The God bestowed blessings that I had just become a second-time home owner five years prior, Ph.D. recipient three years prior and a senior-level leader in the federal government the same year are all due to her sacrifices, her leadership, and our mother to son journey together. Her prayers had been answered.

President Obama's oath of office symbolized the first time in modern history a Black man was recognized as the most powerful person in the World. Inauguration Day, 2009 also happens to have been my mother's 71st birthday. The auspiciousness of this important event was a great birthday present for a mother who knew first- hand, the struggles of an American Civil Rights movement stymied by fear, hampered by distrust, drenched in separatism, and replete with inequality. My mother also knew the joys and benefits of people working together to do what's right. Throughout her life, mom applied effective leadership to overcome mountains (challenges) that would appear unmovable to most people. Her life story is the personification of demanding hard work and perseverance, which serves as a permanent source of motivation for me and so many others.

Just as newly-elected President Obama motivated and inspired a world of people with a platform based on change, my mother provided in life and continues to provide impetus for people to aspire to be effective leaders-people helping people. Her legacy remains the epitome of hope for her biological and surrogate children to cling onto in order to affect change in the world.

How did we get here?

When I first began penning this book, God was working miracles. He had sustained my mother for more than five years since she was initially diagnosed with colon cancer, and I am thankful for each day she lived and each day we celebrated life together. My mother waged a heroic battle against colon cancer that spread throughout her 71 year-old body. Despite the common diagnosis of Western medicine, her faith made the journey just a bit more bearable. Momma Vance fervently refused to allow the wisdom of traditional medicine to defy the power of God. What she taught in life and continues to teach us through her lessons about prayer, purpose, and priorities provides us the strength to share our stories.

Perhaps, there is no greater testimony of prayer, perseverance, persistence and patience than that of my Fraternity Brother Michael J. Jackson. Brother Jackson (R.I.P.) recounts in his book *Prostate Cancer "My Personal Journey"* that colon cancer was no stranger to him because both his mother and aunt had succumb to the deadly disease and provided him the strength to share his story. Brother Jackson traveled the country educating, informing and encouraging cancer patients as well as their friends and family. He was a frequent visitor to my home and a consistent source of comforting uplift to me and my mother prior to her death due to colon cancer.

Recall, my mother and I watched the 2009 presidential inauguration together. We watched the event from home because the frailties of her body would not allow her to endure the enormous crowds, long lines, and cold weather. Danny and Alton were in town at our home for the occasion and were able to attend the D.C. swearing in ceremony. Stage four colon cancer had stripped my mother of those abilities. Her mind was willing, but her body was unable. We were happy and grateful to celebrate the occasion together. Five years prior to the inauguration, I was not sure how long my mother would be around to share any occasions with me, her other children, or anyone else for that matter.

On December 31, 2003, my life, and the lives of everyone who benefited from my mother's existence changed forever. The way I viewed life changed immeasurably. I was now suddenly overwhelmed by the harsh reality of my life-long best friend's mortality. My mother shared with me that she was diagnosed with colon cancer. She told me she had known for some time but was unsure how to share this information with each of her children individually. Faced with shattering the security of so many people who had come to depend on her matriarchal leadership, she did what effective leaders do. She assessed the problem/challenge, evaluated her resources, gauged the emotional intelligence of her organization (in this case her ten children), collaborated and devised a plan of action, executed a communications plan, and delegated tasks to ensure the most optimistic and positive outcomes. She conceptualized the enduring vision. Amazing considering the journey!

Her next steps involved disseminating and sharing that vision with each team member, gaining buy in through trust, assembling small teams to accomplish specific tasks, monitoring progress, and controlling outcomes to the best of her ability.

By now, you may be asking yourself "what in the world does that have to do with the effective principles of leadership" and "how in the world can I benefit from the forthcoming pages?"

Read on.

In the book Enlighted Leadership (1991), the authors posit 'the underlying issue is often found in the soft issues of an organization. The soft issues are the human issues-the fundamental attitudinal or mindset issues of our people. These soft issues consist of less tangible aspects that are much more subjective and less easily measured or charted than the hard issues. In addition, we are less experienced in dealing with these people issues." My mother's medical condition presented our family with a set of extremely difficult challenges and dilemmas that were outside the normal boundaries of our immediate organization's institutional understanding. Once my mother shared the magnitude of the situation, some family members began exhibiting the same dysfunctions described by Lencioni (2012): absence of trust, fear of conflict, lack of commitment, avoidance of accountability, and inattention to results. My mother's condition also raised many legitimate questions and consternations. Most of the questions centered around "what can we do?" and "who will do what?" Fortunately, my mother's effective leadership allowed the team (my brothers and sisters and I) to focus on how to best manage this crisis and how to avert, mitigate, and/or control the physical, emotional, and financial fatigue cancer causes. Once my mother harnessed our energy, we dealt with the soft issues and were able to start dealing with the hard issues. My mother's survival was indeed the primary intended outcome.

In his book, The Five Dysfunctions of a Team, Patrick Lencioni effectively introduces what he describes as dysfunctions teams experience as they form and set out to accomplish specific goals and tasks. He identifies critical human behaviors that prevent groups from becoming teams and illustrates how effective leadership can steer a group toward team formulation. He explains that team work is extremely difficult to achieve, but once realized, companies and organizations become exponentially more productive. Lencioni provides excellent examples of how the five dysfunctions are overcome through effective leadership. More importantly, Lencioni provides practical solutions to what may first appear to be insurmountable organizational problems. Lencioni further explains that once a group overcomes their dysfunctions they can progress as a unit working toward the same goals and objectives with the same outcomes in mind. He provides examples of leadership concepts and behavioral traits people and groups must overcome in order to become a team. These concepts apply to work place environments as well as family situations. By understanding the techniques effective leaders use in order to build productive teams, people are better able to manage projects and leaders are better equipped to lead teams. Maybe Lencioni knows my mother, a mother mentioned in this book, or someone like them.

The Journey

To avert the nearly inescapable oppressions associated with being Black in America, Amelia decided early in her children's lives to expose them to the opportunities afforded by institutions of higher learning. Her story has myriad circumstances lived out through harsh realities. Her unselfish devotion to her family offers an irrevocable deposit to the leadership literature that ensures future generations will never be bankrupt of the first-hand knowledge of the evils of peculiar institutions and the deposits made by mothers to correct the misgivings of male-dominated societies.

One of the most phenomenal entries in her long resume of achievements is Momma V paved the way for her children, grandchildren, great grandchildren, and great great grandchildren to be granted an equal and fair educational opportunity despite limited finances and resources. Her greatest leadership attributes may well be the sense of faith, pride, and dignity she embraced for herself and demanded of those around her. She prayed incessantly!

Leaving Brinkley Arkansas in July 1965, when I was only 30 days old, my mother toted her ten surviving children to Detroit, Michigan under less than favorable circumstances. My father, Aaron Vance, Sr. did not accompany the family for safety/mysterious reasons related to the old Jim Crow South and all the problems that accompany a Black man defending the honor of his wife and family. From all accounts, he (my father) joined the family a few weeks or months later. I have limited memory about the first few years of my life. Here's what I do know. Upon arriving in Detroit, we first lived on Morrell Street in Southwest Detroit, near the rail road tracks under what could best be described as less than ideal conditions. What I do know and recall is we had a host of mothers, aunties and neighborhood matriarchs who were adamant about protecting the 20-30 babies birthed by my mother, my aunt Macie Lee, married to my uncle Comer Bates, Sr., my aunt Faye, married to my uncle James Vance, my father's younger brother, and my God Mother Lizzy Williams, who lived right next door with her husband Preston Sr., her sons Preston Jr. and Gregg, and her daughters Jackie and Bonnie. They were my surrogate God Family.

Are you still asking what benefit you will gain from this powerful real-life compilation of effective leadership stories?

Read on.

My mother's story of survival presents a perfect opportunity and framework to examine leadership from the under-explored perspective of motherhood shaping future leaders. In order to examine and address the principles of effective leadership, I engaged my family and some of my closest friends to share leadership examples from their family, civic, academic, and professional experiences. I also asked them to link those experiences to the lessons they learned from their mothers.

Mothers are the greatest leaders known to mankind!

So, let me state for the record, I acknowledge there is a huge body of work on leadership; from the types and forms of leadership to the attributes and characteristics of leadership (Maxwell: 2007; Wolfe: 2002; Maxwell: 2002; Weisinger: 2002; Walters and Smith: 1999). Most leadership books have common themes which focus on traits like attitude, performance, accountability, integrity, honesty, purpose, and communication to name a few. However, they fall short of offering the exaltations we owe our mothers for the months of labor and years of pain they endure on our behalf. Prior writings also fall short of offering the praise mothers deserve for not only understanding what leadership requires, but for their practical application of leadership principles on a daily, weekly, monthly, yearly, and life-time basis.

According to Maxwell (2002), "leadership" is complicated and has many facets such as respect, experience, emotional strength, people skills, discipline, vision, momentum and timing. My mother certainly perfected those qualities through decades of motherhood. When adding up all the ages of my mother's children, I realized, collectively, my mother had more than five hundred (500) years of mothering experience. Keep in mind I did not include the collective ages of her grandchildren, great grandchildren, great great grandchildren, and surrogate children. Adding all those numbers together, would have given her more than one thousand (1,000) years of leadership experience. With that said, Momma V was a very diligent and experienced leader.

She understood the needs, wants, and requirements of each of her children. She also understood their individual leadership strengths and weaknesses. She understood these things because she instinctively and intentionally invested decades of time, money, emotion, affection, training, and other resources to hone her intelligence about her organization. Isn't that what effective leaders do? Isn't that what effective leadership is all about?

From the time we are born, someone is pulling for us to be the next leader of the free world – whatever that world may be in whatever context. More often than not, that someone is our mother. That is what mothers do. They offer prayer to nurture our minds, bodies, and souls. They suckle us until they believe we are strong enough to face the challenges of the world on our own. Mothers bandage our scrapes and bruises, both physical and emotional, for as long as we need them to. And sometimes longer! Mothers all around the world raise their children to be the very best they can be all the while protecting them from unseen dangers. They raise their children to be embodied with survival and leadership skills. Mothers help us with our homework. They drive us to our band practices and sporting events and teach us lessons in positivity. You all remember the old sayings: "be a good sport", "be a team player", "play well with others", "treat people the way you want to be treated". In other words, these encouragements are the foundation to building lasting partnerships, friendships and relationships built on trust and love. Mothers instinctively provide us with consistent routines like wake-up times, feeding times, bathing times, nap times, homework times, church times, play times, and the like. These are the persistent patterns that comfort us through our developmental stages. These patterns also allow us to recalibrate to our true North Star. What mothers are really doing is preparing our egos to withstand life's challenges and oppositions that we would not otherwise be empowered to handle. Mothers teach us leadership principles like understanding perspectives and setting priorities from the day we are born. Mothers are the greatest leaders known to mankind!

Whether we understand, embrace, or apply the leadership principles we are taught as children plays a significant role in determining whether we become effective or ineffective leaders. I agree with the notion that everyone has the potential to lead if they understand that it does not happen overnight, but requires preparation, patience, and a life time of perseverance (Maxwell, 2002). Effective leadership requires a fundamental grounding in the principles described in this book. I know no one better than our mothers to use as past and living examples of effective leadership. Given the dysfunctional attributes of families and organizations, it is a natural progression for me to draw upon my mother's leadership skills as motivation and desire to move something, change something and advance the causes of other people. Mothers celebrate the strengths in their children and motivate them to develop and improve in those leadership qualities that require strengthening.

I agree that the leadership attributes outlined in the previous paragraphs and explored in past writings are all vital aspects most leaders possess or possessed at some point in their leadership careers. More importantly, I recognize the fact that most successful leaders observed those traits in their parents and/or role models (coaches, pastors, teachers, siblings, etc.) during their formative years. For me, it was my mother and her ability to raise ten children as a single woman with modest means and education that provides the salient, tangible, and enduring leadership examples and lessons I learned throughout life. This book serves as an enabling vehicle to share specific life lessons with a larger audience – you, your family, your friends, and others we have yet to meet. Thanks to our mothers, we can impart true stories about courage, vision, mission, objectives, goals, coaching, team work, and accomplishments. These stories will help you and others navigate the tumultuous roadways effective leadership demands you to travel along your leadership journey.

This book provides examples that show leadership is concomitant with the common bond of people, groups, thoughts, ideas, principles, and causes. The lessons in this book also show that once people, groups, families, and communities embrace and focus their energy on a common set of goals, they can inspire others to join in order to gain Momentum. Once momentum is gained, it becomes a force to be reckoned with. Effective leadership is the foundational framework of Motivation, Optimism and Momentum. **MOM** is an unstoppable force!

Principles are fundamental truths that form the foundation of our individual and collective belief systems. Our leadership principles show up as value systems that determine how we relate to people and processes. The principles exemplified by the mothers in this book project are guide posts for anyone committed to leadership. They are essential to effective leadership and success. The twelve principles included in this book project are divided into three Parts: 1) **Part One** Motivation; 2) **Part Two** Optimism; and 3) **Part Three** Momentum.

Part One of this book shares stories about prayer, positivity, patience, and praise as they relate to the motivation of people, families, groups, communities, and organizations. We encourage you to draw on these principles to become a more effective leader in order to accelerate and enhance your leadership journey.

Part Two shares interrelated stories of purpose, people, persistence, and perspective to provide examples of the organizational skills effective leadership requires.

Part Three focuses on the principles of priorities, preparation, perseverance, and prosperity to provide a formula for building the momentum required to accomplish what effective leadership sets out to achieve-success.

The following pages are filled with examples of sacrifice, commitment, and diligence borne out through the effective leadership of my mother and mothers like her. It is my most sincere hope that this book provides readers actionable examples of the core principles required to be effective leaders in their homes, families, communities, churches, and organizations as they improve their leadership skills and the lives of others who are impacted by their leadership wake.

Be blessed and continue to be the leaders your mothers intended you to be.

Read on!

Part One

MOTIVATION

I n this Part we provide chapters to accompany the various forms of motivation and how leaders can use these stories to motivate those they lead. There is a plethora of ways to describe the age-old concept known as motivation. Weisinger (2002) describes motivations as "anything that arouses one to pursue a particular course of action". Weisinger further posits that "motivation comes in all shapes and forms: thoughts, feelings, a particular word or two, a tangible object, a nontangible need." Motivation is reactant to internal drive as well as external influences or forces. Daniel Goleman (2011) defines motivation as "Being driven to achieve for the sake of achievement with hallmarks that include a passion for work itself and the new challenge, unflagging energy to improve and optimism in the face of failure". While motivation is inspired by responses to internal as well as external forces, effective leadership inspires and motivates people to work together to achieve a common goal. "As leader, your job is to hold the torch of the team goal high, so everyone can see it. But it is also to explain the team goal in terms that the team can respect and respect themselves for pursuing." Effective leaders understand the many forms of motivation and strategically apply them to diverse sets of issues, projects, processes, and people. Robbins and Finley (2004) describe motivation as a means to get people to do what you want by understanding what makes different people tick. One shoe does not fit all. Effective leaders understand different people respond to different stimuli.

In the book, Living on Higher Ground, Paul Lawrence Vann (2005) writes "it is important for us to take a few minutes out of our busy schedules to reflect upon the person(s) or thing(s) that inspired us to leave our comfort zone so we could rediscover the light that led to our success." I often reflect on some of my mother's favorite sayings that are sources of motivation for me. Growing up, mom would always tell us "you can't get anything done lying down or sitting on your butt". She sometimes used more colorful language, but you get the point. Another one of her favorite sayings that resonated with me was "in this life you better get all you can and can all you get". She always motivated us to be the best people we could be today and prepare ourselves to be better people tomorrow. When she wasn't whipping us into shape with words of wisdom and reality, she was shaping our hearts and minds with the Word.

My mother held steadfast to her faith and belief in God's miraculous and awesome powers. My thoughts on motivation are often framed in the context of my mother's uncompromising leadership. Her journey through life and phenomenal experiences prepared me to focus my organizational skills with optimism for helping other people, developing partnerships, and leading, by choice or by default. Naturally, I decided to rely on the leadership skills and abilities of my mother as a source of momentum to navigate the process of imparting this useable knowledge to those who chose to read this book and/or share its lessons with others.

Chapter 1

PRAYER

REGINALD E. VANCE, PH.D.

A
t the time of this book publication, the world was in a vastly different place than 2009. There was nary a person who had not been infected, impacted or devastated by COVID-19 – the Corona Virus. Personally, I was overwhelmed by the passing of one of my best friends, Orville Dale, so many other fraternity brothers, relatives, friends and colleagues due to COVID-19. I paused to consider how I could be of help and service. I also selfishly (maybe more self-preservation) asked how I could get over my personal grief. Reflecting on my original life mission of more than 30 years to help one million people, I pondered what was next. That original mission being completed several years prior, I prayed and asked God to deliver my next assignment. He answered my prayers.

I prayed to God to not only let me and my loved ones survive COVID-19, but to also use me as a vessel to understand this deadly virus in ways that could help others. At the time, I was serving as the Basileus (President) of the Lambda Gamma Gamma (LGG) Chapter of Omega Psi Phi Fraternity, Incorporated–a team of approximately 250 college educated men. Many of them were current or retired military officers, doctors, lawyers, educators, public health officials and community service leaders. During our Saturday February 15, 2020, Chapter meeting, just prior to the wide spread outbreak of COVID-19, a former LGG Basileus and retired military officer, Brother Sherman Charles challenged me and the LGG Leadership Team to lead from the tip of the spear. The words still ring clearly - "Reggie Vance, Tim Worley, Cedric Guyton, Byron Ross, Christian Williams, and D'Ante Byrd y'all need to develop a plan to help curtail the pandemic and help our people however we can". Brother Charles challenged us to be diligent, expedient and outcome driven. The following Wednesday-February 19, 2020, we convened the first LGG COVID-19 Task force meeting to develop the plan to educate our people, inform our people and communicate to our people what we knew about COVID-19 in order to be of service to our communities. That effort led to the Second District (New York, New Jersey, Pennsylvania, Delaware and Maryland) of Omega Psi Phi establishing a COVID-19 Task Force by proclamation of our Second District Representative Brother J. Kendal Smalls and an International (United States, Canada, South Korea, Germany, Virgin Islands, Bahamas, Mexico, Africa, China) Task Force by proclamation of our Grand Basileus, Dr. David Marion. Our 1st Grand Basileus, Brother Rickly Lewis never missed a meeting in more than two years. By God's grace and divine order, I was voluntold to lead at all three levels.

I had to dig deep into all the leadership training my mother instilled in me. Be careful about that which you pray. God answers prayers. I immediately voluntold my dear friend Troy Manigault he was my Right Hand Man. Troy stepped up to the challenge without any equivocation. We stated up front we only knew what we knew and would ask the right questions of the right people to gain a better understanding of what we were facing. By collaborating and listening, we were able to make positive impacts quickly. Brothers Amir Shariff and Kelvin Ampofo were instrumental and very supportive of our efforts to establish the Second District strategy. We also received support from all seven Second District Corridor Representatives (Amir Shariff, Reggie Laster, Damaas Stephens, Delrecole Gaines, Kevin Woodhouse, Avon White, and Ashley Day) Subsequently, we assembled the "Four Horsemen" (Dr. Keith Boykins, Dr. Jedan Phillips, Dr. Cedric Guyton, and Senior Executive Service (SES) leader Wonzie Gardner as preeminent authorities to advise and consult as we figured out our strategic approach to provide information to our Brothers as well as the rest of the Divine Nine and other affiliate organizations. It worked. We provided information, Personal Protective Equipment (PPE) and food supplies to tens of thousands of people throughout the United States and abroad. We continue to experience remarkable success in hard, unforgiving times and will tell fuller stories of our failures (learning curve) and successes in another volume. The takeaway is each of these Brothers were nurtured by mothers and mother-like figures to lead and be responsive to the needs of the people we serve. Simultaneously, Brothers were engaged in keeping their families safe, buying proper provisions, checking on family and friends across the world and shutting down government and private in-person facilities and operations. The tasks were too numerous to name and extremely daunting at all levels. Even the most confident and fearless leader realized prayer was in order, no matter their faith or belief system.

It is axiomatic that we live in a complex ever-changing world filled with diverse people, growing numbers of faiths, beliefs, and religions that inform individuals' spirituality or lack thereof. One constant among those variables is prayer. While figuring out the COVID-19 dilemma, I personally relied heavily on my mother's teachings. While battling cancer, my mother shared a book with me she was reading at that time. In Surviving Cancer (2001) Margie Levine shares "prayer may be effective regardless of religious affiliation, how, or where it is performed, or who actually performs it. Some studies indicate prayerfulness-the act where one surrenders to the great mystery and aligns oneself with the will of God-may be even more beneficial than asking for a specific outcome." Whether or not one chooses to openly admit it, we all pray, have prayed or benefitted from someone praying for us at some point in our lives. For those who do not openly subscribe to a belief in prayer, I submit that prayer is not as vanilla as some people might like to believe. Prayer comes in all sorts of wonderful colors and flavors. So, if you believe yourself to be an effective leader or aspire to the same, I believe your followers will move faster and farther once they associate your leadership with your ability to hope for and meditate on how you achieve individual and organizational success while uplifting others. Hope, optimism, and meditation are forms of prayer. These forms of prayer allow leaders and followers the confidence they need to buy into and complete their personal and collective missions.

My mother was one of the most effective leaders I have ever known. She understood her God given mission. She was also one of the most motivational, prayerful and faith filled people one can ever hope to have known. My mother summoned the courage to overcome her fears so that we (her tribe) might be fortified in faith. Prior to succumbing to colon cancer in 2020, my dear friend and fraternity Brother Michael Jackson (2009) wrote in his book Prostate Cancer: My Personal Journey "The only thing that overcomes fear is faith. Faith is what you need to get you through life's journey. When the doctor gives you a diagnosis like "cancer", you need to know that your faith is strong enough to take you through the healing process." Part of that healing process is know who you are and whose you are. I am and have always been Amelia J. Vance's "Baby Boy". While she prayed for and protected all her biological and surrogate children, no one would argue with the notion that she gave me just a little bit more coverage. She hoped the best for me and others. She remained in constant meditation with the word of God. Before her earthly departure, Momma V shared one of her poems about prayer with me.

God is Just a Prayer Away
By Amelia J. Vance

When Trials and tribulation get heavy sometimes
It seems we can't make it through another day
When friends and loved ones seem to be unkind
Remember, God is just a prayer away

When days are dark and nights are long
No one has time to hear what you have to say
Keep walking in faith; keep your spirit strong
Because God is just a prayer away

Never give up on what is right
Never bow down to the evil that comes your way

Give praise to God both day and night
You know God is just a prayer away

We go through sickness, sorrow, pain, and grief
Sometimes we laugh and sometimes we play
We keep trust in God with much belief
It's good to know God is just a prayer away

So take your trials and burdens to God
Lift up holy hands to him; in his grace always stay
When down life's weary road you trod
You always know God is just a prayer away

God will hear your every word
There is not a time he will turn you away
Every cry: tears and pains he has already heard
Never forget that God is just a prayer away

No other will listen and understand as he
No other can wash your cares away
Whenever we need to talk to a friend
Don't ever forget, God is just a prayer away

My mother taught us to pray at an early age. One of the first prayers we learned was...

> *"Now I lay me down to sleep,*
> *I pray the Lord my Soul to keep*
> *If I should die before I 'wake,*
> *I pray the Lord my Soul to take."*

Still, to this day, I am comforted by that simple, yet empowering prayer. That prayer reminds me we are only here by God's grace and mercy. We are reminded in Hebrews 4:16 "Let us then approach God's throne of grace with confidence, so that we may receive **mercy** and find **grace** to help us in our time of need." That prayer passage also encourages me to do as much as I can for as many deserving people as I can each and every day God allows me to be present in body on His earth. Praying incessantly during my mother's battle with colon cancer allowed me to see things more clearly. Psalms 119:148 laments "My eyes stay open through the watches of the night, that I may meditate on your promises." The simple prayer my mother taught me as a child is consecrated in biblical scripture and gets me through many painful and challenging days. It also guides my decision making process as a leader. It further allows me to better understand my purpose of serving people and placing His plight for my life above my own understanding. It reminds me I can't be the leader I am sworn to be without self-sacrifice and self-abnegation. These are leadership characteristics God wants to see in all His servants. Whenever I say God is good, Taft Gaddy reminds me "God is great; chicken is good." We crack up every time we say that to each other.

Why we pray

Effective leadership requires prayer. Effective leaders understand the power of prayer. My mother taught me to pray at a very young age. She explained to me that prayer is a personal life line to God Almighty and He hears and sees all things. She also taught me to pray with purpose and meaning and not just mouth the words I had learned and memorized. Most importantly, my mother taught me prayer changes things. 1 John 5:14 says, "This is the confidence we have in approaching God: that if we ask anything according to his will, he hears us." Psalms 33:13 tells us "From heaven the Lord looks down and sees all mankind." I personally bear witness to that truth. There simply is no way on earth a little ghetto child from 16th Street ascends from the streets of hard knocks to the C-Suite of civic and private industry without prayer. Prayer changed my life and continues to gird my strength through good times and bad times. The power of prayer allows me to keep my eyes on His prize-helping people.

Tying my shoes

Effective leaders are challenged to consistently motivate others to work together for a common cause. Momma V. taught me that effective leaders are also challenged to organize the collective efforts of others (family, friends, co-workers, and followers) to sustain the momentum that moves causes forward. While writing this book it occurred to me that to maintain the interest and trust of people, groups, and organizations, leaders must summon inspiration from multiple sources. In his book On Becoming a Leader, Warren Bennis (1989) states that "to become a leader, one must know the world as well as one knows himself." Part of knowing the world is knowing people as well as who they pray to and what inspires their prayers. While the drive to lead people to accomplish specific goals and/or tasks can fuel ones motivation for a period of time, leaders often rely on what is tried and true. Prayer! Anyone who has ever tried to teach someone to tie their shoes understands it takes patience, practice, and in the case of mothers teaching their children to tie their shoes, it may take prayer. For me, tying my shoes is a metaphor for the plethora of occasions my life as well as my leadership journey teetered on the precipice of disaster or triumph, based on selecting the right technique and approach to face and make critical decisions.

One of my earliest childhood memories is the day I learned to tie my shoes. It was Easter Sunday 1970. I was about two months shy of becoming five years old. My mother had been trying to teach me how to tie my shoes for several weeks, if not months. We would practice a few times a week. For some reason, I just couldn't get the hang of it. I could see the frustration on her patient face. She never got angry. She never scorned me for my lack of aptitude or acuity. She just kept helping me. I almost gave up. She never gave up on me and she wouldn't allow me to quit. Many times we would just take a break and pray for a breakthrough. I believed in my mother. I trusted her prayers. I didn't want to let her down.

One Sunday morning, I kneeled with my mother at the side of her bed in prayer before we set off for church. My mother prayed aloud for many things such as food, shelter, and clothing for her family. She prayed for a safe environment in which to raise her children and grandchildren. Then she prayed in silence. When we were done praying, I asked my mother what she was praying for in silence. She responded, "that's

9

between me and my God". Not one to miss an opportunity, I asked my mother if I could say a special silent prayer too. She told me "as long as you pray with your heart, God will listen and answer your prayers." So, I did. I prayed in silence for a minute or two. When I opened my eyes and unfolded my clinched praying hands, my mother asked me what was my silent prayer? Well, if you know me, you know how I responded. Of course…Momma, that's between me and my God. I also braced myself for the backlash, only to receive a huge hug and hearty laugh. Yes, I got my sense of humor and quick wit from Momma V. Soon after, we set off for the Holbrook Church of Christ that morning as promptly as we had always done for as long as I could remember. My mother instilled a sense of promptness and responsibility in all her children. It started on Sundays.

When we returned from church, I retreated to one of my hiding spaces underneath the stair well on the first floor of our house on 16th Street between Popular and Buchanan on the West Side of Detroit. That house seemed so huge to me at five years old and I found many places to escape and hide from the world. Interestingly, in her book *My Mother's Rules*, Judge Lynn Toler (2007) shares how she would retreat to a closet in her house for solace and how her mother discovered her hiding place and coaxed her into facing and overcoming her challenges. What her mother did for her shaped who Lynn Toller is today and is another example of instinctive motherly leadership. Like Lynn, I experienced a day of epiphany on Easter Sunday due to my mother's coaxing.

I climbed onto some boxes and reached for one of my mother's church hats. Not just any old church hat. This one was bright and vibrant and had a huge bow on it. This was the right hat. This was the right opportunity. This was the moment. This was it! This was the moment that all the training, practice, and praying would finally culminate. That morning, I had silently prayed to successfully tie my shoes and now it was time for me to find out if God had been listening. So, I threw caution to the wind and stepped out on faith or blissful foolishness. I gently untied the bow from my mother's spectacular church hat, carefully calculating how to reassemble the bow. They call it reverse engineering these days. I prayed that I wouldn't totally mess up that front pew, Easter Sunday church hat beyond repair. From the perspective of a five year old, I believed that if I could untie that bow and tie it back on the church hat, I could use the same process to tie my shoes. It worked!

I untied and retied the bow for practice and untied and retied the laces on my knock off brand of gym shoes that were purchased from the local discount store. That day signified a pivotal moment in life for me. The success I achieved immediately elevated my mother from momma to life-long Leader in Chief in my mind. That life changing event gave me confidence to follow her and her vision wherever it would take us. I was no longer just momma's Baby Boy. I felt like I could lace up my shoes and be part of the team. I could be self sufficient and take a small burden off her plate. I felt accomplished. Momma V had done her job as a leader. She instilled in me hope, optimism and confidence.

Throughout life, my mother instilled in me a sense of faith and re-minded me of the power of prayer. I have also been blessed with coaches, teachers, co-workers, and other family members who have exemplified their belief in the same. However, we often fail to fully understand and respect the power of prayer until something dreadful happens in our lives. Paul Lawrence Vann (2005) tells a dreadful yet inspiring story about the power of prayer and how prayer helped sustain him and his family during his mother's illness. Vann recounts how for thirty straight days he visited his mother in the hospital and prayed for her every day until she passed away peacefully in her hospital bed. Despite the hard-ship and tragedy of the situation, he found motivation in the faith his mother instilled in her children. Their family stayed together and prayed together. Their belief in the power of prayer was unwavering. All effective leaders should aspire to this level of higher consciousness.

In 2004 my family faced a daunting reality similar to what the Vann family faced. Collectively, we realized our mother was not promised tomorrow, much less the number of years we all selfishly hoped to share with her. My family faced a major crisis, unlike any we had ever known. The question for me was rather I would allow myself to succumb to the depression and despair brought on by this new reality or would I follow in my mother's footsteps and find the strength to summon the motiva-tion and intestinal fortitude required to meet and defeat my fears. The broader question was "how do we as a family, deal with this crisis?" Hiding under the first floor stair well was not an option.

Edward M. Kennedy (2006) writes in his book America Back on Track "like" so many families, mine has not escaped the tragedy of disease or pain of injury. More than forty years prior, in his book, Profiles in Courage, John F. Kennedy (1964) wrote "the Chinese symbol for crisis is the symbol for danger combined with the symbol for Opportunity." The passages from the Kennedy brothers were prophetically sobering for me. Through prayer and eternal optimism, I learned to view my mother's cancer diagnosis as an opportunity to be supportive of my mother as well as an opportunity to lead by example. I prayed fervently that God would have favor on my mother, her children and those who loved her and cared about her. I prayed that sibling rivalries would be extinguished in order that we might focus on the intensely heated mission at hand. I prayed that my mother would live to see many more years without the stresses levied on her by her adult children. I prayed that my brothers and sisters could all find it in their hearts to do what was best and what was right on my mother's behalf. I prayed that God would give me the strength to galvanize the efforts of family members, doctors, nurses, and other medical attendees to make my mother well. I prayed that we could all pray together despite our differences. I prayed for the same things my mother had always prayed for. I prayed that once we did all we could for my mother, we all would be able to accept the triumphs as well as any impending defeats. I'm sure you and others in this world have prayed for similar things. So have our mothers and mother-like figures-the engines that drive our success.

Surrogate Mothers and Sons

The date was February 28, 2009, which happens to be the birthday of one of Momma V's surrogate sons, Orville Dale (rest in peace). I awakened my mother to prepare her for the weekly blood work regiment and medical treatments we had become accustomed to experiencing. I asked a question which had been on my mind and heart for some time. I asked Momma V how was she able to be so strong in the face of such adversity as raising ten children on her own, providing for countless others, and now fighting the most fearsome battle of her life? In her usual faith-based and spiritually grounded responsive manner, she replied "I just keep praying and God keeps answering my prayers." Momma V provided me similar encouragement from childhood through adulthood as I had received from Orville's mom-one of my surrogate mothers, Mrs. Agatha Loiuse Dale (rest in peace). Momma Dale passed away May 16, 2004. Coincidentally, my father Arron Vance, Sr. passed away May 16, 1999, just five years prior. My sister Coletha reminds me God deals in numbers and I am finally beginning to grasp and embrace that concept. If you are from Detroit, you know how we like to play the numbers. LOL!!!!

Momma Dale always treated me, my brothers and all the kids in our neighborhood as her own. We were all in that number of extended family members subject to constant love, nurturing and grooming. She saw our leadership potential before we even knew how to spell the word or fully comprehended the impact of our leadership skills. Even in our early years and going forward, there was never a time those mothers mentioned and who will be mentioned did not open their doors to the broader community. Momma Dale was a fervent prayer warrior who led by example and instilled a sense of confidence in everyone she touched. We were truly a village. The concept of family and village allowed us to be leaders in our neighborhoods, sports teams, college campuses, jobs and civic engagements. Mrs. Dale always exhibited a stern yet loving and comforting demeanor. She also had a sense of what was going on in the home as well as the "street." We dared not embarrass our family at home or in other places.

Once Orville and I returned to Detroit from college, Momma Dale made sure we stayed focused on our careers and always had elaborate Jamaican meals for us to consume while sobering from long weekends customary to young twenty something year old men finding their way in life in the early 1990s Detroit environment. She never missed an opportunity to support our business ventures and instill basic "good people" and sound leadership character skills. Similar to Momma V, Momma Dale moved to Detroit in the late 1960s to pave the way for her family's future prosperity. Momma Dale eventually was joined in Detroit by five children (Beverly, Carl, Lorna, Althea, and Orville). Mr. Rupert Dale (one of my surrogate fathers) joined the family in Detroit a short time after Momma Dale. Her sacrifices are truly the epitome of servant leadership. Momma Dale was a true leadership pioneer and her legacy lives on with multiple generational leadership stories to share. She believed in prayer. She believed in us. Our successes could not have been realized without her constant prayers. Thanks Momma Dale.

On Thursday, April 23, 2009, my mother passed away and was laid to rest the very next Thursday, April 30 (seven days later). Serendipitously, my best friend of 30 years, Steve Dunbar, one of my mother's surrogate sons, passed away April 30, 2016, exactly seven years to the day we laid Momma V to rest. The two dates will always be challenging for me. I actually questioned God on several occasions and asked why would He place such a heavy burden on me (just plain old selfish and short sighted on my part). After much soul searching, I reconciled to continue loving, caring and leading in order to help as many people as God, life and time allows. While Steve and Momma V were absent in earthly form, they were present in spirit. More importantly, the lives they lived deserve to be documented and their legacies deserve to be carried forward. So, our true family and friends came together to make sure their lives would not have been lived in vain. Even to this day Momma V's annual memorial continues and Steve's wife Chaunceia (Carter) Dunbar and many of Steve's DJ and House Music/Hip Hop aficionados are working diligently to establish a non-profit organization to honor his leadership accomplishments as well as help others on their leadership journey. We owe it to Momma Dunbar to continue the Dunbar family legacy. We will get there together through persistence, patience, and prayer.

Similar to the Momma V and Momma Dale stories, Momma Dunbar-Mrs. Kathryn Johnson Dunbar was yet another village matriarch weaving the tapestry to develop strong young men and women along their leadership journeys. Interestingly, the Dunbar family moved to Detroit the same year as the Vance family, 1965. Steve and I were born the same year three months apart and were destined to achieve remarkable things together. While attending Southern University in Baton Rouge, Louisiana, Steve orchestrated legendary parties and I maintained the books. Momma Dunbar instilled a sense of leadership and entrepreneurship in Steve, his older brother Morris Dunbar II, older sister Anna Mechele Dunbar, as well numerous surrogate sons and daughters. I am confident her prayers and comforting advice contributed greatly to our leadership journeys and successes through college and well into our adult lives.

The last year Steve and I spent as roommates at Southern University, at the urging of Momma Dunbar, she and husband Dr. Morris O. Dunbar, Sr. (one of my surrogate fathers), actually purchased a minivan to transport Steve from Detroit to Baton Rouge. The minivan was filled with household goods and food provisions. Once arriving in Baton Rouge, Momma Dunbar and Dr. Dunbar made sure we had adequate housing, the cupboards were full and we had what we needed to have a successful school year. They only had a few demands of us. The first demand was we go to class and maintain good grades. The second demand was we take care of each other and hold each other accountable. A third demand was we stay focused and prayerful. Momma Dunbar was preparing us for life after college and equipping us with essential principles all leaders must possess. There are so many motherly nurturing stories we can share about Momma Dunbar. She supported our academic pursuits at Southern University. She always made sure we had home cooked meals when were home from school and she definitely held our feet to the fire when it came to making the right career and life decisions. Just as our faith has been girded by prayer, it was prayer that allowed our mother's children and surrogate children to step into leadership roles in order to build upon their leadership legacies. I'm not telling you what I heard. I'm telling you what I know.

Prayer is powerful. Prayer changes things. Effective leadership requires prayer. Please keep praying for your leadership success and the success of those you lead.

Chapter 2

POSITIVITY

REVEREND MARCUS HILLIE

I t is impossible to know my mother and the mothers in this book and not have some understanding and appreciation of the power of being positive. No matter what challenges they face, it is rare to hear mothers with valid leadership perspectives verbalize negative thoughts, actions, or words. Margie Levine (2001) reminds us to stay positive, persistent and persevere. I aspire to ascend to that level of positive thinking, positive actions, and positive endeavors. We reflect on the Book of Romans (Rom.) to start the dialogue on positivity.

We are reminded to "Rejoice in hope, be patient in tribulation, be constant in prayer."(Rom. 12:12); and "Let us rejoice and hold fast to positivity through the trials and tribulations of this world. Give thanks and stay positive, knowing that God will protect and deliver us from evil and despair as we are faithful to Him." Sing songs of praise and glory to God!

"May the God of hope fill you with all joy and peace in believing, so that by the power of the Holy Spirit you may abound in hope." (Rom. 15:13)

In 1966, the legendary songstress, Dionne Warwick recorded the landmark tune, "What the World Needs Now is Love" for her album entitled, "Here Where There is Love". Included in the lyrics of the tune is the verse, "What the world needs now is love, sweet love; No, not just for some, but for everyone." When we pause to consider all the pain and turmoil that swirls around, and through our daily lives, it would appear to be difficult to understand how one might keep their spirits lifted and heads held high, in the face of adversity and the mounting pressures of life. One attribute of effective leaders is the ability to invoke positivity in diverse and complex situations. The ability to exhibit positivity empowers team members to look at a half empty glass as a half full glass. The best leaders motivate their followers to view the glass as always being full. While liquid may occupy and account for a portion of the content in the glass, air is always present above the water line - the surface. That's where leaders allow their followers to breathe in order to make life surviving decisions. When applied properly, leaders model behaviors that provide hope, optimism and confidence that embolden members of their organization to believe they can navigate choppy waters with a sense of fearlessness. Even the poorest swimmer can stay afloat long enough for help to arrive. That help avails itself in the form of prayer, positivity, patience and praise.

Left to our own devices and devoid of the spirit of love, we look for this affection in all the wrong places and often find ourselves in precarious predicaments that our creator never intended for us to experience. We live in an instant gratification society where our every desire, including food, entertainment, banking, and companionships can be arranged by the touch of a finger through our respective electronic devices. The news cycle is 24 hours long and people live and die due to cyber bullying and stalking. I echo the phrase, "What the World Needs Now is Love, Sweet Love." With love, there is no hate; with love, there is no deep-ceded, systemic racism; with love, there is no police brutality or rampant drug trade in our respective cities across these yet to be united states. I take refuge in the fact that God is real, and Jesus is Love. When I look back over my life and think things over, I can truly say that I've been blessed. This reminds me of one of my favorite scriptures from the Holy Bible. In Psalm 23:1-6, the prophet David professes "The LORD is my shepherd, I lack nothing. He makes me lie down in green pastures, he leads me beside quiet waters, he refreshes my soul. He guides me along the right paths for his name's sake. Even though I walk through the darkest valley, I will fear no evil, for you are with me; your rod and your staff, they comfort me. You prepare a table before me in the presence of my enemies. You anoint my head with oil; my cup overflows. Surely your goodness and love will follow me all the days of my life, and I will dwell in the house of the LORD forever."

The Lord provides for us when we find ourselves in the deepest of valleys and He showers us through windows of blessings that were not expected. The world has adopted the colloquialism that God is my co-pilot; but the fallacy in this statement is that no one, person, place, or thing can ever be in the position of being equal to God. If God is your co-pilot, this means that you are sitting next to God, and you are equally navigating your pathway. It is God who leads me beside still waters and allows me to lie in pastures of peace. We, by ourselves, cannot keep our heads about us when others are losing theirs and blaming it on us, but with God, all things are possible. I serve a God who sits high and looks low. I serve a God who promised never to leave me or forsake me. He has restored me and forgiven more of my sins than I can remember. He continues to lead me on the path of righteousness for His namesake. I take no credit for the joy that I have for I exist strictly by the grace of God. My life is a living testament to the soul saving power that rests in His hands. He didn't have to call me out of darkness and allow me to bask in the glory of His marvelous light. He didn't have to save me from the hounds of hell, BUT…He did. I count every trial in my life joy, for in my struggle, God is glorified.

Therefore, I can walk through the valley of the shadow of death and not fear any evil for God promised that He would be with me. The blessing in the text is that the Word says that we walk THROUGH! The valley is not my destination, it is a pathway *through* the shadow of death. David said in the midst, of my enemies God will prepare a table for me and that my cup will run over with His blessings. Lastly, the text advises that God's goodness and mercy will follow me ALL the days of my life. How could I not be encouraged by the promise from God, the creator to me, His creation. We are bombarded daily with the worries of the world. These worries range from ongoing squabbles between our elected officials to insurrectionist who seek to re-shape government to facilitate their self-serving interest. People ask me how do I keep my countenance lifted in light of our station in life and the world in which we live. My joy, my happiness, and my peace come from the love of God and His everlasting grace and mercy. The love of God liberates us from the shackles of sin, illuminates us when we are in dark places, and elevates us to higher levels of spirituality. Positivity leads me to praise God for the work He is doing in my life and the blessings of family and good friends. Yes. What the World Needs Now is Love, Sweet Love.

Chapter 3

PATIENCE

Reverend Dwain Harrell

I t's often said that the first step to fixing a problem is admitting you have one. So, as a disclaimer, I admit that patience is not one of my better qualities. Oakley and Krug (1991) challenge leaders to deal with the real issues and not merely the symptoms of a problem. They recognize "many organizations tend to deal primarily with these symptoms time and again, rarely digging deeper to find their source". Bill Gates says "success usually comes after a lot of trial and error and a lot of failures. Successful individuals are those who have the patience to stick through all the frustrating moments along the way." Being frustrated is a temporary experiential symptom and natural progression for effective leaders. The passion is there. The commitment is there. The care is there. As leaders, just like our mothers, we want the best outcomes as soon as possible. If we are astute, we recognize our mothers instill these coping mechanisms in us from day one. It is up to us to use those mechanisms to be better leaders for those who follow us. Balancing our passion, commitment and care as leaders can make all the difference in our leadership journey.

As with symptoms of physical illness, if the doctor merely treats the symptoms and doesn't treat the cause of the problem, the symptoms persist or return. Understanding and embracing my leadership and life style,

I have committed to addressing my lack of patience and offer readers scripture that will assist them on their leadership journey. The drive and demand for survival coupled with my competitive nature causes me to constantly balance success and empathy. Whenever my competitive drive to complete tasks starts to overtake my affection for people, I immerse myself in my mother's journey.

The Power and Blessing of Patiently Waiting on God

Developing patience can be one of the most difficult aspects of a Christian Life. One of the key questions we must ask ourselves is while our patience is being developed, "what do we do in the meantime and what do we do while we wait?" In this chapter I want to focus on the life of Hannah and what Hannah can teach us about the power of Patience.

Hannah was the wife of Elkanah a man of wealth and influence. However, Hannah has a big problem. Hannah was unable to conceive or bear a child. To add insult to injury, her husband Elkanah took another wife name Peninnah who bore him several children. Now Peninnah went out of her way to make Hannah feel inferior about her inability to bear children. Now Elkanah loved Hannah and always gave her a double portion of blessing while at the offering. Yet despite Elkanah's kindness, Hannah was heartbroken about her inability to become a mother. One day, her despair got the best of her and while in the temple she cried tears of bitterness and despair and pleaded with God to grant her a child. She promised God that if she had a child, she would dedicate the child back to the Lord. Faithfully, the Lord heard Hannah's plea and allowed her to conceive a son, which she named Samuel.

1. Waiting on the Lord requires we patiently trust God enough to be honest about our issues and challenges.

What Hanna teaches us is while we are waiting, we must have the courage to patiently trust God and to be honest with God about our issues and challenges. This is clearly reflected by Hannah in Sam. 1:10. In her deep anguish Hannah prayed to the LORD, weeping bitterly. Hannah had waited patiently for years for a child, but when she went to the temple, she didn't pretend things were okay, she was experiencing deep sorrow. Yet, even in her waiting and despair, she knew she could trust her heart to God and that and God had the power to address her needs. Like Hannah, we will face many issues and challenges, while we wait patiently, we don't have to bear our issues alone. While we wait patiently, we summon the courage to lay our transparent feelings before God. No matter how dark our thoughts or how discouraged we feel, we can take our honest and transparent feelings to God, He already knows our heart and what we need before we even ask.

2. Waiting on God requires we patiently - Trust God and His Timing.

There is a saying the "He may not come when you want Him, but He is ALWAYS on Time". That leads us to our second point, like Hannah, we must "Trust God's Timing". When we look back over our lives, I am sure each of us, at one time or another, felt God was moving too slow and taking His sweet time. Like Hannah's heart ached for a child, we too have felt like what we ache most for took the longest time to come to pass? For you see, it's in the moments of our lives that are filled with sorrow, hurt and pain, that God uses to stretch our faith and draw us closer to Him. In these dark and dismal moments, when we can turn to no one else, that is where we discover the true meaning of Trusting God. Like Hannah, we will discover that when our heart is truly broken, that is where we truly learn to wait on God's timing and Trust in His plan, even when we can't track him. While the days may seem long, God is never late and delivers His promises at just the right time. Waiting on the Lord allows God to do his work and is worth the wait.

3. Waiting on God requires we patiently – Build our Spiritual Strength by fervently and faithfully seeking God.

Hannah taught us one final powerful lesson about waiting patiently on God. That lesson was that during our darkest hours, we should never stop praying and seeking God. Hannah did not let her inability to bear children, hinder her relationship with God or keep her from seeking His face. Hannah knew that despite her situation, her relationship with God had to keep growing while she patiently remained in the waiting room of life. Even if you don't feel God's presence or have become fatigued during the waiting process; our best defense during our times of challenge are to seek God's Face, Read His Word, Render our prayers and never forget His Promises in Scripture.

While we don't know how many years Hannah waited on the birth of her child, what we do know is that during the process of patiently waiting on God, she faithfully and fervently sought after God. While Hannah could have thrown in the towel and accepted the fact that she would never bear a child, that thought never entered her mind. Even amidst ridicule from Peninnah, Hannah faithfully and fervently sought after God. For her steadfast faithfulness, God met Hannah and answered her prayer. This should remind us that even when we are at our lowest points in life, as with Hannah, God will meet us and give us the endurance we need to press on. No matter what problem lies ahead of you, no matter what dream or vision seems out of reach or even dead, please remember the story of our Sister Hannah. Let her example of honesty, transparency, trust, and faith in God motivate us to hold on to God's promises during our times of Hardship. As with Hannah, let us patiently Trust God with our issues, Trust God's timing, Trust God's Plans and Pathways. Let us build our spiritual faith as we patiently wait on God to move on our behalf, just as He did for Hannah. As God answers each of our prayers, let us remember the Blessings and Benefits that come when we patiently wait on Him.

Chapter 4

PRAISE

Dr. Kwamme Anderson

Merriam Webster defines the transitive verb praise, "to express a favorable judgment of commend". In its noun form, "an expression of approval: commendation; worship; value, or merit." (Merriam-WebsterDictionary.com, 2021).

When I think of praise, what immediately comes to mind is my formative years growing up as a tot in the syrupy sweet town of Natchez, Mississippi. Nestled along the banks of the second-longest River in the United States, the mighty Mississippi, its namesake is attributed to the Natchez Indians. Since its 1716 establishment, Natchez has been along a major trade route and now, in the 21st Century, is a historic site claiming 700,000 tourists annually (ms.farmcountry.com, 2009).

There was much wonderment for a child living in the southwest quadrant of the state that borders Vidalia, Louisiana. My very first memories of learning to whom praise was attributed to as an object originated from my mother, around the tender age of three. One day, while sitting on my twin bed, she asked, "Kwamme, do you know what prayer is?" Without contemplating I readily answered, "yes, Momma, prayer is talking to God", which she confirmed, "yes Baby, you can tell God anything you'd like". Fast-forward 43 years, I still stand on that same foundational tenant.

My home church, Jerusalem Baptist, was located at 608 S. Wall Street. Every Sunday, rain, sleet, snow, shine, or sans absence, we would arrive beforehand at 9:30 a.m. promptly for Sunday School. You could bet on my father to make sure were always present, and timely. His motto, *"I would rather be one hour early than five minutes late"*. This helped to instill within me a moral compass that perpetually guides me unto this day.

At Jerusalem, we learned weekly, who was worthy of our praise. My understanding of who The Most High God was reinforced throughout both pre-kindergarten and elementary school, at Holy Family Catholic. As strict as they were, the Nuns were equally loving - religiously incorporating Mass as part of our academic curriculum. Synergy abounded between home and school to help give me an undergirding for days like these.

The basic elements for our moral building blocks makes for an unwavering, fundamental internal constitution. Upon immediate recall, my parents taught me two major lessons: 1) to thine own self be true; and 2) treat others as you would want to be treated. Down through the years, these mantras have helped define my raison d'etre. It helps keep me keenly focused on running the race that is set before me.

Also instilled within me was the exhortation of others. And, to give credit where it is due. This makes for good sisters, brothers, friends, and neighbors. Complimenting you on your light does not diminish mine. Conversely, I innately believe it strengthens us in an unforeseen place that stirs up the gifts in you, and me. For this, it is one of the main reasons why we were created — to give praise to The Most High God, as well as to encourage one another with words of commendation.

Within the confines of the framework, Herzberg's Theory of Motivation (Herzberg, 1959), this vignette will focus on the internal and external sources humans need to feel inspired, satisfied, and more productive. Specifically, those two factors are: 1) hygiene and 2) motivators. Directing our attention to motivators, Herzberg postulates that humans need recognition for their achievements in the workplace. This in turn, inspires employees to feel more job satisfied, rousing them towards reaching the penultimate goal of increased productivity.

While applicable to the work environment, it is just as relevant to our personal lives. Whenever you have the opportunity to commend someone, take the time to give them credit for their efforts, or even express the meaning of their being in your life. Here, you can directly exercise praise, either in writing, or verbally. Praise helps others to feel good about themselves, validates their humanity, and motivates one to keep moving forward or even, to keep up the great work.

Let's face it - life is hard. There is no standard operating procedure or instructional manual we can readily refer to with real-time assistance to handle its vicissitudes. Okay, forgive me Millennials and Digital Natives, there is Google. But even with its millions of searches within the nanosecond of a click, it still leaves gaps and cannot answer every need. That is why as humans, we should pride ourselves in contributing to the overall health and well-being of mankind. As His creation, we owe our all to the Creator by rendering Him praise. In concert, we owe it to our fellow brothers and sisters to speak affirmations of motivating upliftment because one never fully knows the extent of what a kind word will do.

Keep on praising!

Part Two

OPTIMISM

I n this Part we share how mothers' optimism permeates throughout the organization and serves as a catalyst to engage and empower those they lead- their children. Each contributing author posits their personal experiences and their mothers' life-long attention to purpose, people, persistence and perspective – those traits shape their leadership journeys.

According to Psychology Today, "To many psychologists, optimism reflects the belief that the outcomes of events or experiences will generally be positive. Others contend that optimism is more an explanatory style; it resides in the way people explain the causes of events. Optimists are likely to see the causes of failure or negative experiences as temporary rather than permanent, specific rather than global, and external rather than internal. Such a perspective enables optimists to see the possibility of change more easily."

How do you view optimism and how do you apply the concept to your leadership style?

My mother was the eternal optimist. There is an indelible impression that will be forever etched in my mind. When we were kids, still living on 16th Street in Detroit, Michigan, me and four of my siblings attended Kennedy Elementary School, just a couple blocks away from our home. According to the principal and our teachers, we were all bright kids. While we excelled in the classroom academically, we could be a bit rambunctious. So much so, they hired my mother as a school aid. I believe that was one of three jobs she worked simultaneously to keep her children and other families in the neighborhood afloat and relevant. Her optimism would not allow us to fade into nothingness. Assigning my mother as a school aid paid off for the school, her children and the countless other children she reached.

Our school books were old and we did not have readily available access or transportation to libraries, where we could access historical and relevant knowledge. We were certainly economically disadvantaged but were not to be dismissed or discarded. Not just the Vance's, but most families in our neighborhood. So, how would we keep up with our peers in better neighbors? My mother sacrificed and figured it out.

Before there was an internet replete with social media, google and other search engines, there were these book volumes called encyclopedias. Salespeople would visit neighborhoods and make payment arrangements with families who could or could not afford the books. Don't know how she did it, but her faith, hope, and optimism lead her to believe her children and others' children had purpose and would remain persistent in their quest for knowledge. Not only did she acquire the encyclopedias for her children, but she also made sure they were available to any neighborhood child who needed them. We kept those books for a long time.

The preceding is just one example that is still replicated and repeated by so many mothers in so many neighborhoods, communities, cities, states, and countries around the world. We challenge you to consider how optimism can improve your leadership journey.

Chapter 5

PURPOSE

CASHENNA CROSS

The idea of purpose sets the scene of great expectations and wields a massive amount of awkwardly guilty pleasure. In the book *Enlightened Leadership* Oakley and Krug (1991) state "whether working for a Fortune 500 company, a professional baseball team, or an entrepreneurial venture, an internal bred purpose (the reason for which something exists or is done, or an intended result) clarifies direction and fuels the fire of achievement." Lorin Woolfe (2002) suggests that we all need purpose in on our lives. She writes "Work without purpose (even if it takes great skill) can become mindless heartless drudgery. Add purpose, even to so-called grunt work and our work lives take on an expanded, even inspired dimension"

Once upon a time… a statement in and of itself equals expectations. The introduction sets the scene for the reader to dream to ask the questions, to wonder. Yet, no one ever stops reading at "Once upon a time." No; we continue. We continue to see if the ending based on the book/ novel/play's title actually builds to the fruition of the readers expected conclusion.

As the writer of this chapter let it be known that there is an acknowledgement that true purpose comes with hearing of, reading about, and experiencing the world around us. What about those who "never left their backyard" so to speak? How will they discover their purpose? See, broaching the subject of purpose can be perplexing. Its complexities rest in the unknown and discovering the essential criteria that leads us to discover our purpose internally, externally, locally, and globally. However, in many ways, it is simply having an expectation. Why am I here in this moment and what will I do with the time I am given? There it is! Purpose is congruent with achievement and accomplished by planting a seed of EXPECTATION! The Bible is clear that we were created by God in order to bring Him glory. The ultimate purpose of man (humanity), therefore, is to glorify God (Isa. 43:7). We are to know Him and make Him known [to others who do not yet know of him] by glorifying Him with our lives. Now PURPOSE just got easier for those who read the Bible and know God- we live to glorify him. Boom, living for Christ Jesus, Amen! Now, what of the unbeliever who additionally is part of making the world go around and around? For whom are they living?

The idea of purpose has even the author of this book on a journey. In turn, the offer of the following three recommendations is a present help in shaping purpose.

1. Believe YOU are A-amazing,
2. Speak your truth into reality, and
3. Keep visualizing or dreaming of you[r] **complete** [ion].

Each has a proven measurable level of success towards this author's understanding of the unseen, the unknown and hope in the future.

Believe YOU are A-amazing!

YOU. Y – O- U, you. Turn it into a country love song. You are amazing a record which should play so frequently in your head until it breaks the sound barrier of negativity endured daily. Embrace awkwardly guilty pleasure. Some might believe embracing awkwardly guilty pleasure is just bragging, you lack self-sacrifice. NO! The idea isn't to be arrogant or puffed up, but it's biblically noted that sometimes you have to encourage yourself. Do not be anxious about anything, but in every situation, by prayer and petition, with thanksgiving, present your requests to God. (Phil. 4:6) It's the petitioning with thanksgiving which gives the courage to be fully sure that as God's creation, formed in his image that he who knows all things – with that knowledge resides within in the fruit of the tree cleansed through the blood of his son Jesus Christ. How (A to Z) amazing is it to read that your purpose is that of the omnipresent Lord. Wow!

Truly don't you want to believe in the best visualization of you? Try going to the grocery store and say, no I don't want that unblemished apple. Yeah, I'll have the one with the wormhole and the one the kid just kicked across the floor. Yep! That's the apple for me. Laughable right? Or at least folks will think you are a little peculiar. NO you want the apple the produce manager just polished, the one gently soaked in sprayed water; so that it glistens as you turn it against the light. The crown jewel which makes you stay–blocking others from getting their apples until you're finished selecting your best. So, why is it that awkward guilty pleasure exists when we present our visionary selves up before the light? Number one stop it! Stop feeling lost, and displaced. Believing you are A-amazing and in the type of RIGHT NOW space makes positive things happen because you are there. Once you believe you are amazing, the purpose wheel turns for others as well as you. When you give amazingly it can very well open doors once closed. Lightbulb! Often times your purpose isn't about the grand ole finale for you exclusively, rather miniature sound bites of life successes which paints that purpose in full tapestry. Give yourself over to believing in the amazing you and see won't the day present a level of clarity to suffice the actuality of purpose. The purpose of giving God the glory is that: GOD DON'T MAKE NO JUNK! That's what my Momma said, and I choose to believe her and the WORD. So be the hero of your own story and live the life of distinction because the potter (God) has excellent clay (you) hallelujah! You are A-amazing because God said so when he sent his only begotten son to save humanity. (Believer and the unbelieving) "Therefore go and make disciples of all nations, baptizing them in the name of the Father and of the Son and of the Holy Spirit, and teaching them to obey everything I have commanded you. And surely I am with you always, to the very end of the age." (Mat. 28:19-20)

Speak Your Truth into Reality

The power of life and death is in your tongue and those who love it will eat its fruit. Life and death are in the power of the tongue, and those who love it will eat its fruit. (Prov. 18:21) The tongue can bring death or life; those who love to talk will reap the consequences. So let your talk be of good report - that's some real ownership only you possess. Purpose is modestly in part what you say it is. Clearly no human no matter the age says I choose to be *(insert the negative words of your choice)*. No. Purpose allows this author to stand on the greatest oak tree branch and say everyone starts from I am *(insert the positive words of your choice)* and I want to be a *(again insert your positive professions)*. Then where does speaking go wrong? When outside influences press in on all sides, finances, stress, depression, age, and other factors produce negative energy that causes us to lose sight of our divine purpose.

We often hear the stories of homeless children succeeding and going to Harvard or Yale. The once abandoned creating healing solutions speaking life to orphanages and leading mission trips abroad. Purposeful living it would seem is tied so genuinely to the speaking of truth. As we say it, so shall it be. It's critical to speak wealth if you're strapped for cash. To speak of serenity if you are stressed. Clear your mind to speak of healing if you are depressed. Age is just a number. The greatest case in point, remember although Abraham was incredibly old, Sarah conceived and bore a son in her old age too, at the time that ***God had foretold*** her a son Abraham called Isaac which in Hebrew means laughter. (Gen. 21:2) See God spoke life or purpose into existence. Isn't it ironic that name Isaac means laughter, because Sarah did think it funny that God should have her, a well in age old woman bear a child? (Gen. 18:12-15) So she laughed to herself, saying, "After I am worn out and my master is old, will I now have this pleasure?" And the LORD asked Abraham, "Why did Sarah laugh and say, 'Can I really bear a child when I am old?' Is anything too difficult for the LORD? At the appointed time I will return to you—in about a year—and Sarah will have a son." But Sarah was afraid, so she denied it and said, "I did not laugh." "No," replied the LORD, "but you did laugh." Now that's powerful. You must speak life to your purpose. You must speak the essence of God-like breath to your dreams regardless of your present day circumstances. Today is not the tomorrow which

God has in store for you. God said: "Before I formed you in the womb I knew you, before you were born I set you apart; I appointed you as a **prophet** to the nations." (Jer. 1:4-5). A prophet, a person regarded as an inspired teacher or *proclaimer* of the will of God. Do not stop speaking the vision, never stop speaking life to your determinations. Then watch for the manifestation.

Keep Visualizing or Dreaming of Your Completion

Visualizations help us to consolidate the various desire of life into one succinct track. There are thrusters which kick start the energy of a once straight path into different paths or directions, but all will necessarily generate a focus point to keep your eyes on the goal if you utilize the power of visualization. The power of visualization is able to spread the wealth of the possible from idea to spoken word, to action, to completion. Take action in accordance with (Habakkuk 2:2) which says, "And the Lord answered me: "Write down the revelation and make it plain on tablets so that a herald may run with it." When it is written down and then implemented, those we lead including ourselves can "run" with it and we will see it succeed. A clear process begins to develop when the plan is made plain, simple and basic. Don't over think it. The written word like the spoken word commits you to work towards it. Like forensic science, once you write the vision you own it as always being attributable to you. No pressure. Truly, it is no threat to dream. Dreaming is the expectation of wholesome benefits for a good cause. (You are that good cause that is well worth it)

The dream world serves to restore and refresh you to appreciate the hope within. Feedback from the dream world may too be scary, but a deeper understanding of the message of the dream can clean up many unanswered questions and in certain cases be just in time feedback. The Bible indicates that God revealed His will to selected people through dreams or visions in scriptures such as (Gen. 37:5-10); (First Kings 3:5-15); (Dan. chapters 2 and 7); (Mat. 1:20, 2:13-19); and (Acts 10:9-16; 16:9). Remember, Joseph's interpretations, two dreamers (Gen. 37:6), two of his fellow prisoners in Egypt each have a dream (Gen. 40:5), and Pharaoh has a pair of dreams (Gen. 41;1-7). The first pair sets the narrative in motion (one prisoner freed, one prisoner beheaded) and points ahead to its destination. Again the purpose of interpreting the other prisoner's dreams leads to Joseph's purpose becoming even clearer and another step closer), while the second and third pairs are catalysts for Joseph's eventual ascension and yet another purpose borne out of the evil done to him by being sold into slavery by his own brothers to being in position to save them from starvation during the famine. There's a clarity which comes with the visualization process but carefully check any such guidance with scripture and additionally trusted counsel to be sure it is a word held especially for you. (Second Tim. 3:16-17) shows that God has revealed His will to us primarily through His Word. It says, "All Scripture is God-breathed and is useful for teaching, rebuking, correcting and training in righteousness, so that the man of God may be thoroughly equipped for every good work." Where there is no guidance, a people falls, but in an abundance of counselors there is safety. (Prov. 11:14) Repeat, in an <u>abundance</u> of counselors there is safety.

Dreaming at night or day is not only healthy scientifically, but it also gives purpose. The sum total of purpose is again miniature sound bites of life lived and yet to be lived. The sound bites together make the picture reality - so the more dreaming the merrier. As a child day dreaming "having a sense of wonder instills a genuine smile and breathe energy in the thought of "it's possible" or "it could happen." Why loose that? Daydream more with a mustard-seed sized portion of faith - remember the carefree existence it gives us to visualize ourselves; as complete, as victors.

Ultimately, to really understand purpose is to simply live with both your eyes wide open. Ears ready to hear, and positive affirmations in mind and heart despite the odds. Why? Because (Mat. 24:36 says) "But about that day or hour no one knows, not even the angels in heaven, nor the Son, but only the Father. No not a one of us should know of the second coming of Christ, the end of the world, and the last judgment. As such, purpose isn't really branded until it's materialized aka hindsight we can appreciate. My advice then on purpose is keep a positive get-up-and-go attitude, strive towards tomorrow by living your best life today. Moving the mission FORWARD: believing YOU are A-amazing, speaking your truth into reality, and lastly keep on visualizing or dreaming of your achievement as if it's already done - because it is. Truly I tell you that if anyone says to this mountain, 'Be lifted up and thrown into the sea,' and has no doubt in his heart but believes that it will happen, it will be done for him. (Mar. 11:24) Accordingly, continue to realize your life's book weighted against the goals and wildest dreams of your life's maturation surpassing today's reality by tomorrow's expectations day after day.

Like many people, you might feel that you're simply existing in life, going through the motions without understanding what it all *means*. In *The Purpose Driven Life*, Pastor Rick Warren reveals the meaning of life from a Christian perspective—five purposes that you were created by God to fulfill: worship, unselfish fellowship, spiritual maturity, your ministry, and your mission.

In living for your purposes, you'll start to find meaning in every moment of your life. You'll learn to see the glory of God everywhere, deepen your love for others, find the unique service you were *made* for, and prepare your character for the promise of eternal life.

And we know that in all things God works for the good of those who love him, who have been called according to his purpose.

Stay prayerful. Remain positive. Maintain your patience. Keep praising.

Chapter 6

PEOPLE

BILL MINIX

P eople were made to be in communion with one another, and to be companions, friends, and of service to each other. People are the means by which purpose is achieved, and every individual you meet is uniquely equipped with special gifts and talents that are intended to add to your life to improve it. Two people never come together by accident; it is always a divine rendezvous. However, most of the time we mistake the collision for something other than what was intended, and we miss the assignment. We were created in the image of God to know, love, and serve Him. Likewise, we are expected to respect, love, trust, and serve other humans and our encounters with one another should have no less consideration than our preparations to encounter God himself. Now let's explore how mothers' model successful leadership attributes.

Terry R. Bacon (2006) posits "your success and the success of your group or organization depend to a great extent on your ability to build effective relationships with people you manage." People will embrace or reject your leadership based on your consistency or inconsistency in displaying genuine concern for other people. It is accepted that the abilities to motivate, inspire, and persuade are three characteristics of effective leadership. These are lessons that mothers teach instinctively as they model the success that each of us should have when engaging other people. These and other lessons are manifested behaviorally in caring, sharing, and assurance. As I reflect on the leadership lessons that Maggie Minix taught me, think of your own mother or mother figure that nurtured and loved you unconditionally. This image will help you understand the degree in which you are expected to give of yourself to others.

Mothers teach us how to care and share and leaders soon learn that people don't care how much you know until they know how much you care. Caring is observed in a mother's behavior from the moment she learns she is pregnant. A mother will adjust her diet and stop consuming things that she likes to avoid harming her unborn child. Mothers who are impoverished and face the difficult decision of eating first or feeding their hungry child will care for the child first. So, sacrifice is a leadership trait that mothers teach and real leaders consider those they serve before themselves. As a military officer, my soldiers always ate before I did, and if rations ran short, I simply "made do". Today it is quite the contrary as I listen to many CEOs of failed companies rationalize accepting millions of dollars while their people lose their jobs, and individual retirement accounts. Many executives in healthy companies also seek to maximize their bonus structures and stock options while minimizing salaries, benefits, development, and privileges of their employees. I'm often drawn to Covey' (2004) and his assertion that "a principle-centered person thinks in terms of effectiveness in dealing with people." Serving self is not a mother's principle, it's not a biblical principle, and it's not a leadership principle. Leaders demonstrate that they know how to care and share through giving of their time, talents, and resources.

Mothers are also inspirational and excellent motivators. They nurture children through the developmental stages and encourage them to crawl, walk, and run. Daily they coach their young to eat right, talk right, and play right. Repeatedly they reinforce positive messaging by saying "you can do it" and when done, their genuine expression of gratification radiates throughout the very essence of the child. They inspire repeat behavior and continuously coach children to higher levels of success. The result is a child excited about learning and eager to explore and conquer the next adventure. Leaders are charged with the same task of motivation and inspiring the people they serve. Unfortunately, society does not teach leadership and people mistake strength, power, control, and high individual achievement as indicators of good leadership. There is a tendency to look to those who are loud, demanding, and critical of others for leadership examples. As you endeavor to enhance your personal leadership, learn from your mother's excellent examples. It was her tenderness, kind words, and positive reinforcements that inspired you. Occasionally she had to be firm to reinforce your learning about consequences for both good and bad behavior, yet she always managed to return to a motivating and inspiring state. She did not have to get loud to let her seriousness be known, and her eyes and facial expressions were enough to signal her power and control. The consistency of prior teachings made clear the expectations and my siblings and I were glad to course correct behaviors instantly to meet mom's high but fair standards. Her power and influence was best illustrated through her meekness, and not through her might. Her inspiration and motivation was driven by her trust in her children to do the right thing. Leaders believe faithfully that your people are capable of marching toward your vision and achieving purpose and they will. Hold them accountable for their actions with a genuine interest in reinforcing the right behaviors and they will run through walls for you.

Many mothers believe in the biblical advice, "Fathers, do not exasperate your children; instead, bring them up in the training and instruction of the Lord." (Eph. 6:4). In the same way leaders are expected to teach their people how to perform." The mistake that most make is they simply want to tell their people what to do and expect that they will gladly do it. To train mandates personal involvement of the leader. To tell is shunting responsibility. Leaders, be the example of highly effective leadership that you want your people to become.

May God continue to bless mothers all around the world for their excellent examples of love that all leaders should endeavor to possess.

Chapter 7

PERSISTENCE

DR. IRA CREDLE

"I say unto you, Though he will not rise and give him, because he is his friend, yet because of his importunity he will rise and give him as many as he needeth." Luke 11:8 KJV

All Glory to God

I once heard an old preacher say whenever you stand before the people of God to speak, the first thing out of your mouth should be acknowledging Him. Thus, I use the same mindset in writing, for if it had not been for the Lord, who was on my side, where would I be. My mother was married as a teenager to a fellow neighborhood teen under less than favorable circumstances. After her mother coordinated an arranged marriage, that man would be the father to her five sons. My mother, Rebecca Ann Credle (White) finally got the courage to divorce him a couple of years after her last son was born. Ironically, she never planted seeds in her sons that would ferment hate towards our father and with her outward expressions of forgiveness, who were we not to forgive him. To his credit, although he was never a father to us, I personally fostered enough of a relationship with him that led to him being a descent grandfather to my daughter. Following the divorce, my mother mustered enough money to purchase a trailer and was allowed to place it in her mother's front yard off to the side of the property. She quickly moved from a domestic to an inspector on a line in a textile mill and with the village led by two amazing grandmothers, it appeared we were transitioning from survival mode predicated on government subsidized foods to creating options for a future of potential possibilities. In the book Think and Grow Rich (1937 and 2015), Napoleon Hill submits "There is no substitute for persistence! It cannot be supplanted by any other quality! Remember this, and it will hearten you in the beginning, when the going may seem difficult and slow." My mother was persistent.

My Leadership Journey

The year 1976 was the worst year of my life. I broke my elbow playing in the Turkey Bowl that November. My paternal grandfather died in October. While returning home from the tobacco field, I broke my ankle jumping off the back of a pickup truck before it came to a complete stop. I was devastated because the next day was August 1st—the first day allowed to start high school football practice. I was already a late bloomer and the consequences of a year deferred resulting in me playing junior varsity my junior year. The worst of the year came a few months earlier in April. Having my 15th birthday on the 12th of April was a blur in my life because what occurred in the month of April 1976 was one of the most significant emotional events of my life. My mother had taken us (me and my two younger brothers) to my youngest brother's fourth grade play. My oldest brother who was a great linebacker, but a more prolific hurdler in high school, decided to drop out of college and join the U.S. Navy to take some of the financial burden off our mother. The next to the oldest had started college at Saint Augustine's College in Raleigh. By the way, that's the same college attended by Orville Dale who Dr. Vance mentions earlier in this manuscript. As we returned from the play, we started to enter the James City (subcommunity of New Bern, North Carolina) area and instantly noticed people walking and cars lined up along the side of the road leading all the way back to near where we lived. One may have thought that a major sports event was occurring under the circumstances. As she slowly navigated the vehicle passed parked cars and the many pedestrians walking to the scene, she would occasionally ask someone "what's going on". No one knew or at least wanted to say. We finally got to the end of the road where the fire trucks became visible. We could all see the trailer going up in flames. My mother had recently paid her brother to build a little porch with a cover, so you no longer had to walk two flights of stone stairs to enter the trailer, but everything she had worked for and everything we owned was burning at that moment. By the time we got out the car, the firemen had gained control of the fire. If you want to learn more about persistence as you continue on your leadership journey, continue reading this impactful chapter and powerful collection of stories about how mothers influenced the successful leadership journeys of their children and others.

We were allowed to walk pass the smoldering carriage structure that once held our home when suddenly, my mother's knees buckled, and she went down to the ground. My two younger brothers and I immediately lifted her back to her feet as we entered my maternal grandmother's house. It was an awfully uneasy feeling for us all. I had watched her work so hard and now it was all gone. I would not have that real sense of fear of the unknown for another 15 years as I would be leading an artillery firing battery into combat during the Gulf War. My maternal grandmother, Mrs. Tempie White, was a domestic and didn't have much, but she made up for it with love and the sharing of her wisdom and words of encouragement. One of her sons had managed to get that house built as the previous old two-story home was dilapidated and eventually torn down. As we sat there in a valley of despair, I didn't think nor did I have the capacity to pray, but what was revealed to me was the power of a mother's prayer during difficult times and how God's love for His faithful followers is manifested as we go through the vicissitudes of life.

My snuff dipping paternal grandmother was a retired educator who single handedly kept us out of total poverty. If the cupboard was bare in the trailer, we could always go two dirt roads over to her nice two-story home and find something in the refrigerator. I know for a fact, she did what she did for us because my father was not doing anything, but also like my other grandmother, she genuinely loved us with all her being. As we sat in a confused state, not knowing our future, Freddie Hall Credle, pulls up into the yard with her green Chevrolet Caprice with a tan vinyl roof. She was short in stature and her head appeared just over the steering wheel. Because it was night, she was still in her "house coat" and bed clothes. My grandfather was her passenger and stepped out of the vehicle. He stood about six feet or so but seemed taller that evening. He spoke as he entered "Momma Tempie's" screen door and immediately looked at us three boys with total calm and confidence and simply stated - "come on y'all, everything gonna be alright". It was his finest hour for me. He would pass of a second stroke later that October.

In the book of Luke, chapter 11, verses 5 through 10, Jesus poses a scenario to his followers. Suppose you have a friend, and you go to him at midnight and ask him to lend you three loaves of bread for another friend of yours who has come from out of town. The account goes on to describe the friend on the inside telling the other not to bother him. He has already locked the doors and his family is asleep. Jesus tells them that the man does not get up to give his friend the bread because of their friendship, but his audacity to have the nerve to wake him up at that hour. The King James translation uses the word "importunity" which Webster describes as pressing or urging with troublesome persistence.

I watched my mother work hard every day to raise her five sons while living in a trailer in James City, NC. All five are college graduates and some with multiple degrees. Their work experience range from Federal Government to International Business Machine (IBM). In 2000, my mother retired from Cherry Point Marine Air Station where she worked as an inspector on an assembly line that refurbished blades for the Presidential Marine One helicopters. She was talked into buying a 3-bedroom rancher in 1989 and paid it off in 2017. She was once asked what she attributed to her sons being productive citizens and she replied, "they were determined". I wonder where they got that. (Luk. 9-10) reminds us to ask and it shall be given to us, seek and we shall find; knock and the door will be opened. For all who are persistent in asking the Father will surely receive the Holy Spirit to guide them through any adversity. With the help of the Holy Spirit my mother prayed, directed, and motivated her sons to be men of character, not perfect, but men who honored their mothers and are respected in their own right.

If you are a leader or aspire to be a leader, my message is simple. We all endure hardship and don't always know why things happen. What we do know is God does not place upon us more than what we can handle. Let the lessons of your mothers and mother-like figures be your inspiration to be good people and greater to other people.

Chapter 8

PERSPECTIVE

Reverend Ademuyiwa Bamiduro

It's interesting how people react to crisis and how they view their circumstances. Robins and Finley (2004) share a very interesting perspective on perspective. They write "All work is meaningful and worthy of respect, even if you work in a pickle plant. You can be carrying a hod of bricks or you can be building a cathedral – the meaning is all in your perspective." Perspective shapes the way we perceive our assignments in life. As leaders, we must muster the strength to make the best of even the worse situations so that those we lead maintain a sense of purpose and commitment to fulfilling the collective goal.

Recently, I received a phone call from my mother. Unlike other calls to check on me, this call was to deliver some not so good news. She called to tell me that she had been diagnosed with cancer. The news hit me like a ton of bricks. My mother, who had single-handedly raised my two older siblings and me following the unexpected death of our dad and her husband, had now been diagnosed with a terrible disease. Although my mother's news about cancer was heartbreaking, it was her next statement that reminded me of her humanity, her leadership, and her God-given perspective. Immediately after breaking the bad news about her cancer diagnosis, my mother said: "well I'm glad that I am getting this diagnosis now when you and your brother and sister are grown and can take care of yourselves." Her perspective was sobering; it was encouraging; and it reminded me of Godly wisdom. Her perspective personified the strength of a matriarch's leadership.

The Cambridge dictionary defines "perspective" as "a particular way of considering something" or "to think about a situation or problem in a wise and reasonable way." Perspective is directly connected to making decisions, and decision-making is a critical component of leadership, particularly during difficult and challenging circumstances. And for many, including my mother, perspective and decision making is tied to faith. Noted actor Eldred Gregory Peck once said that "Faith gives you an inner strength and a sense of balance and perspective in life." Through faith, mothers have demonstrated leadership not only within the home, but in all aspects of society including in corporate American, academia, philanthropy, and entrepreneurship.

The connection between faith and perspective and leadership principles can be seen in the biblical narrative about a mother's encounter with Jesus in the Gospel of (Mat. 15:21-28). There, we are told that Jesus and his disciples are in Tyre and Sidon, a Gentile region considered unclean and despised by the Jews. While there, a Canaanite woman demonstrates her faith in Jesus when she approached and repeatedly asked Him to help her unwell daughter. Although Jesus heals the woman's daughter, it is the conversation with Jesus and His disciples that reveals this mother's faith-based perspective and the following leadership principles: (1) operating in uncomfortable environments; (2) anchoring persistence in prayer; and (3) trusting God.

First, the Canaanite mother's faith-based perspective led her to operate in what had to be an uncomfortable and unwelcoming environment. As a Gentile from the vicinity of Tyre and Sidon, the odds were stacked against her. She was disliked, considered unclean and unfit, and yet she made the decision to approach Jesus and His Jewish disciples, the very people who viewed her with scorn and reproach. The disciples demonstrated this disdain when they urged Jesus to send the mother away because she kept "crying out" for help after them. No compassion, no concern, no kindness. Despite the difficult and discouraging circumstances, not unlike conditions many of our mothers have had to endure, this mother demonstrated sage perspective by not retreating or giving up.

Instead, she pressed forward with perspective and a rich understanding that deliverance is often born out of discomfort. Perspective leads to operating in uncomfortable environments, and unwelcoming conditions often foster character and leadership.

Next, this unnamed Canaanite mother's persistence in her pursuit also revealed perspective. Importantly, her persistence was anchored in prayer. Although we are told from the disciples' response that the mother kept crying out after them for help, the entirety of her words are unreported. Three of her statements are however recorded, two of which confirm that her persistence was anchored in prayer. To be sure, here initial request to Jesus, "Lord, Son of David, have mercy on me! My daughter is demon-possessed and suffering terribly" And her second statement (made while kneeling before Jesus), "Lord, help me" are both prayers. Persistence anchored in prayer provides clarity for the pursuit and confirms the path. Simply put, prayer offers direction and protection. Leadership can and is often difficult, and perspective is to acknowledge that a consistent connection with God through prayer produces strength, comfort, and encouragement throughout the pursuit. The Canaanite mother, like our mothers, appreciated that prayer makes a difference and is necessary when seeking to overcome challenges, including discrimination, sexism, and obstacles that threaten the wellbeing of their family and children. Leaders who maintain a prayerful resolve reap the rewards of perspective.

Lastly, Jesus's response to this mother also gives us insight about her perspective. Jesus initially responds to her pleas for help with silence. Jesus broke his silence at the urging of His disciples to send her away, but only to tell the mother that He "was sent only to the lost sheep of Israel [,]" and thus not the Gentiles. This mother nevertheless persisted in asking for help, to which Jesus said, "It is not right to take the children's bread and toss it to the dogs." Again, the mother pressed forward and replied, "Yes it is, Lord, . . . [e]ven the dogs eat the crumbs that fall from their master's table."

Commentators differ on the meaning of the exchange between the mother and Jesus, but the mother's perspective was evident by her trust in God despite unfavorable circumstances. Jesus's initial hurtful silence combined with His cutting statements confirming the derogatory labels associated with Gentiles could be perceived as unhelpful. Perspective however prompts the reality that God's ways and thoughts are highest. In uttering those statements, Jesus acknowledged the common thoughts associated with Gentiles. But Jesus does not stop there. He then recognizes the mother's faith and heals her daughter. Thus, not only does Jesus highlight the wrongheaded notions about Gentiles, His healing of the daughter through the mother's faith confirmed that there is no room for such discrimination and evil in His kingdom. The mother's perspective to trust God even in the face of hurtful and demeaning conditions led to her acceptance and her daughter's healing. But for her perspective to trust God, His power to help the mother overcome trying times and to break down barriers may not have materialized.

Our mothers trusted God. And their trust in God aided their leadership and as a result they witnessed God's provision and blessings. They overcame unimaginable pain and suffering and remained resolute because they had perspective. Their perspective and leadership have been felt throughout history, including nurturing generations of children and adults who also positively impact our world. Perspective can be the difference between successful and failed leadership. Thank God for our mother's perspective.

Part Three

MOMENTUM

This part – **Momentum** rounds out the **MOM** acronym – the essence and anchor of this book project. My mother intrinsically understood the power of **M**otivation, **O**ptimism and **M**omentum. At age 27, with ten children in tow, she visualized how collectively the three concepts had the ability to help her children and others. In 1965, Amelia J. Vance made a conscious decision to move her children out of the Deep South Arkansas cotton fields to an industrial Detroit full of hope, optimism and potential. WOW! That's bold by any standard. Momma V set her priorities and stuck to them. As we shared earlier, my father Aaron Vance, Sr. would later join the family/organization in Detroit and find work as a brick mason. By all accounts, he was great at his craft. There is still an old school barbeque pit at the Vance Kentfield property in Detroit that is functional and has been used for over forty years to bring family and friends together. That's a significant return on investment. What I learned from my father is bricks are foundational and money matters. My mother often joked that her **"Baby Boy"** still has the first penny he ever earned. I got my sense of money and finance from my momma and my daddy. While I don't quite know where that first penny is, I do know the whereabouts of that first dollar. We will talk about that in the final chapter- prosperity. Thanks Brother Pirtle!

I often jokingly tell folks when I was 30 days old, realizing all my siblings and relatives were picking cotton, I asked my mother to pack my brief case and important papers so we could move from share croppers to share owners. That's my metaphorical and hyperbolical account. My mother's boldness and forward thinking shaped my leadership journey. The truth is my mother employed her leadership skills to get us out of a tragic existence and afford us opportunities to dream, live and achieve. Her preparation provided us with the momentum to move forward in the manner best suited for each individual member of her organization. She knew each of us better than we knew ourselves. She took a personal interest in each of her team members' wants, needs and aspirations. The best of leaders learn how to do this over time.

Max Landsberg (2002) does an excellent job connecting effective and inspiring leadership to vision, inspiration and momentum. Consider the term "momentum" outside the academic discipline of physics, as applied for example in the realm of politics. If a presidential candidate sees a gain in public-opinion polls then wins a debate and embarks on a whirlwind speaking tour, the media comments that he/she is "gaining momentum." As with momentum in the framework of physics, what these commentators mean is the candidate is/will be hard to stop. To carry the analogy further, he/she is doing enough of the right things (thus gaining "mass"), and doing them quickly enough, thereby gaining velocity. Their commitment to perseverance is paying off.

The faster an object moves —whether a baseball, an automobile, or a particle of matter—the harder it is to stop. I had the advantage of bouncing my ideas and thoughts off my dear friend Sugar Ray Bullock (rest in peace), an upper classman while I attended Southern University on this matter. He helped me understand how to simplify and socialize the word momentum in the context intended for this leadership manuscript. For many years, Dr. Bullock served as an academic icon at several Historically Black Colleges and Universities (HBCUs). He also served on grants evaluation teams for federal government agencies. Because of Dr. Bullock, I have a deeper understanding of momentum. Thanks my friend.

Chapter 9

PRIORITIES

DONALD MCKEEVER

Dwain Harrell is one of the authors to this book project and happens to be one of my Omega Psi Phi Fraternity Brothers. In his book Uplift (2021), he provides a very prophetic entry into the leadership dialogue as he observes our country is more divided than any of us would have imagined in 2020 based on our politics throughout our workplace, within our families, and of course our religion. He suggests that making the right choices at the right time, as we see them, determines how we set priorities in our lives. In the book The Accidental Leader, Robbins and Finley (2004) share an example of how one can solve problems sooner than they expect by understanding the importance of prioritizing and selecting the right task to address at the right time. Setting priorities. I believe most mothers around the world make the right decisions at the right time instinctively to protect and preserve their families and communities. Mothers who master the ability to understand and embrace emotional intelligence, reason and rationalize, set aside immediate self-gratification for the long-term health and stability of their organizations are some of the best examples of tried and true leadership.

This chapter is dedicated to all mothers for their unconditional love and support. Quite often I am reminded of the unique tone my mother asserted when she spoke. This authentically creative method of communication was meant to keep us in line. However, there were times when my brother and I behaved inappropriately to the degree that it required being firmly disciplined by our mother. Many times, after a short physical encounter that seemed like hours, she would follow up by saying "You better get your priorities STRAIGHT!" Our priorities were as straight as they could be for a seven and ten year old who were clueless and naive to life.

What I now realize, almost 50 years later, is that my mother was planting a seed that would inevitably grow and nurture children, grandchildren, and additional generations for years to come. The "seed" of priority would be tested, debated, and adjusted as time moved on.

Priorities are important and for members in our family, everyone understood my mother's concept of priority because it was coupled with expectations. In chapter six of this book, Mayor Cashenna Cross shares how setting expectations coupled with priorities helps us realize great achievements. In the McKeever household, one of our primary goals as a family was to establish priorities as a foundation to build toward success and constantly evolve. In the Book Primal Leadership: Learning to Lead with Emotional Intelligence, Daniel Goldman et al (2002) writes "goal-oriented planners get what they go after." If my mother's goal was to produce two men to become active positive contributors to society, she achieved what she went after. If you want to know more about how mothers instill the priority principle to help their children and others navigate their leadership journey, please continue reading.

Let's take a moment to understand what a priority is by definition. According to the Merriam-Webster dictionary, a" Priority is something given or meriting attention before competing alternatives". In our daily life encounters, we are confronted with issues and circumstances that place us in a position to make decisions. This is the moment when we should choose wisely and prioritize accordingly. It is important to note there are factors such as personal experience, finances, opportunity, and timing that influence one's ultimate analysis and decision-making process on matters small and large. Napoleon Hill posits procrastination is the enemy of effective decision making and the most prosperous leaders are those who are capable of reaching decisions in prompt fashion and not succumb to procrastination.

For example, consider your daughter has enrolled in college and lives more than 1,000 miles from home. She calls and says, Daddy I need an additional $500 for campus housing expenses. In an effort to have an enjoyable and fun time, you planned a night at the Casino. Of course, the $500 allocated for playing pleasure at the casino will undoubtedly be sacrificed in order for your child to secure housing. However, consider the same scenario as previously mentioned with time being your friend. The payment is expected within the next two weeks for housing. Now an opportunity has presented itself to continue with your desired plans at the casino. In this instance, each goal has the probability of being met. Here we can see that timing plays a significant role in prioritizing.

I believe most people agree the basic essentials of life-food, clothing and shelter are universally the top three priorities for human beings. However, there are people who have chosen a variety of activities that put those very essential things in jeopardy. Statistics compiled by the Addiction Center estimate that about "21 million Americans have at least one addiction but only 10% of that number receive treatment". Many of the addictions whether it be alcohol, opioids or sex have put everything they have worked for at risk to feed their addiction, even if it meant losing everything else. Choosing what will take precedence and actually living your life accordingly is a very difficult task, but it will certainly help you along your leadership journey when you make the right choices at the right time. Prioritizing is more difficult if you never really take the time to consistently acknowledge and meditate on your true priorities. Since the birth of my twins eighteen years ago, I have been on a personal journey to refine and redefine my approach to setting priorities. I optimistically hope this chapter inspires others to take steps to make a list of their top two or three priorities and take action to achieve success. I recommend you start by asking yourself this basic question "what are my top priorities?" Now write them down and measure your progress.

I would have to say "Faith" is my top priority. This is true for people of religious affiliation and those who believe in a higher spiritual being, Faith is more than likely the most significant factor that guides a majority of my decisions. We hear of astonishing stories and people with extraordinary talents that almost seem unimaginable. We sometimes refer to these 'GIFTS" as "GOD GIVEN"! For those of us that have conquered the unconquerable, lived through unbearable circumstances, witnessed the unbelievable, we all attribute these events as being capable through GODS grace and mercy. My true belief is events that occur daily are all small parts of a much bigger picture. This motivates me to try to make decisions not only to better myself as a person but to also make decisions that will ultimately help and provide for others. It is through my Faith that even the negative things that I experience can somehow be a message that maybe I should approach something differently because that challenge was in some way a message that I may be going astray from God's will. We have all heard the quote by Napoleon Hill (1937)," The body achieves what the mind believes". Hill spent more than twenty years studying successful people and concluded among other attributes, desire, faith organized planning, persistence and perseverance were keys to individuals achieving wealth and prosperity. This I have to believe is the essence of why Faith is my most important priority. My nurturing from a small child always included emphasis that we should always strive to do our best with our GOD GIVEN talents and if we confessed to try and serve his will that our lives would be fulfilled with Blessings. I believed it then and I believe it now.

My family is probably my second top priority. My own definition of family extends beyond my direct bloodline. My family also consists of individuals whom I have identified as having a genuine care for me that is stronger than a common friendship. These individuals are the people I trust with my inner thoughts, feelings, and future plans. Even though my immediate family does take precedence in most situations, my extended family is also very important to me. I believe it is imperative that the knowledge and experiences that I capture in life should be shared with my family to help guide them through situations that they will also experience. My mother and father would always let my brother and I know that all of their hard work was to make a better life for us. They constantly reminded us that their hard work would ultimately allow us to experience a better life than they had and we should in turn want the same thing for our legacies to come. It is important that you build a strong foundation with your family so that the things you worked so hard to accomplish, spiritually, morally, and materialistically can be passed on to future generations.

Last but certainly not least, my third priority is management of my time. Timing is everything. It is important to use your time wisely and also respect others time as if it is your own. Once time passes you can't get it back. No one feels good about engaging in any event that they consider a waste of time. Perfecting time management will create many positive opportunities. How many times have you received an unexpected blessing just because you happened to be at the right place, at the right time?

I can remember in college when I was pledging to gain membership in my Fraternity, we were taught the 5 P's. Proper Planning Prevents Poor Performance. This was advice that I have tried to live by ever since. It simply means that if you take the proper time to plan out anything that you do, your results will usually come out better than if you don't.

Thus far this has worked very well for me.

In conclusion, Priorities are important in setting a foundation to live your daily life. Priorities will change based on many different circumstances. Establishing Priorities and letting others know what your priorities are helps one focus on those things that are important and allows you to utilize your time wisely.

Chapter 10

PREPARATION

ANGELO RIDDICK

A Lesson on Leadership - The Foundation

"Get up! Men don't lay around all day. Find something to do!" I hear those words everyday no matter the day of the week. My grandmother heartily enforced the rule and would often express the command with vigor and contempt for those who would otherwise let the day go by. What she was instinctively and intentionally doing was teaching me life lessons about preparation. In chapter seven of Think and Grow Rich, Napoleon Hill suggests organized planning and preparation are keys to future success. Like so many others who grasp this concept, I understood at an early age what my grandmother was instilling in me and I appreciate how her efforts contributed to my successful leadership journey.

Ms. Beatrice-S. Harris (Ms. Bea) raised me. She adopted my young mother who was blessed with twins at the early age of 13. She wasn't ready for my brother and I but "Ms. Bea" stepped in and filled the gap. Her rules were exact. Reny (my twin) and I followed them explicitly without complaint. She, like so many others at that time, worked as a domestic housekeeper who not only cleaned houses but took care of the kids of mostly Jewish clients. They had a way of subordinating her but she did not yield or reduce herself to inferiority while sheltering us from the same.

The 1960's were as turbulent through the eyes of children as it was for all who knew the rules and either tried to enforce or resist depending on your color at the time. My grandmother would shop downtown in my hometown of Norfolk, Virginia every week. Sometimes we'd venture to the shops and stores in what was referred to as "uptown" and other times we'd go to the mainstream shopping area distinctively in this case referred to simply as downtown. For Virginians it meant, the "white" shopping districts.

Not understanding the protocol of the day, my grandmother would strangely refer to obviously younger white shopkeepers as sir or ma'am and the reverse was the norm uptown. Shopkeepers would give deference to her age in those shops. Afterall, she was 60 years old at the time of my birth and her seniority was obvious to all but those people who ran the shops downtown.

Ms. Bea sheltered us from the civil angst by doing things that were hard to understand through the eyes of a child. She always carried a collapsible drinking cup and dutifully fetched water when we (Reny and I) complained of thirst. She would never let us venture to a fountain for any reason. She would also present a humble manner to everyone but would not bow down to subordination at any turn. I distinctly remember the repetitive lessons of demeanor and kindness no matter what the environment. Her strength showed through literal humility and her dignity was never compromised.

It took more than 30 years for me to understand her actions at the local Woolworth. Ya see, at some point she would take us to the Woolworth centrally located on Granby Street in downtown Norfolk. This was the only place she never used the word "no" to any request my brother and I would throw out. We'd sit at the counter and study the menu. She said yes to everything we asked for no matter the cost and at the end of each meal she'd allow us a treasured treat, the coveted banana split. During that time, banana splits were a novelty of sorts. After ordering, patrons would select from a bouquet of balloons fashioned at the end of the counter. The price of the split would be predicated by the balloon that one chose. A small price tag was sealed in each and the prices ranged from one penny to 75 cents. We'd get to choose and could count on this treat whenever we visited downtown.

It took years to realize that my grandmother was simply enjoying a recently gained freedom of the civil rights movement. She was not a vocal advocate of the movement nor was she a weak woman who stood for any indignity of the time. She simply displayed a strength in character that was stern, understanding and most of all humble and she taught and reinforced those lessons to us in everything she did from making sure we rose before sunrise and tempered our manners when we interacted with elders. Her strict rule was to say yes sir and no ma'am to anyone who appeared to be 15 years in age or older. She reinforced all rules with the "hand". There was no "spare the rod" thinking in our house. From her, I learned determination, kindness, humility, and the value of dignity. Lastly, I learned that there were no limits to my future despite the changing times.

Before I share my understanding of leadership from the lessons learned in my grandmother's house and the values therein, I want to illustrate how she taught me to dream. Each time we'd walk to the big grocery store literally seven blocks from our house in Park Place, we'd pass an Old Dominion University fraternity house still positioned in what was an old stately neighborhood that slowly "blackened" with time. In the early 1930's it was a redlined neighborhood that was off-limits to blacks but slowly opened up when a delipidated slum was torn down near downtown. Obviously the first resident understanding the value of this future shift in demographics, decided to rent a house in Park Place to a black tenant, and white flight took off. The frat boys, however, didn't get the memo and maintained their Omicron Chi fraternity house at the very fringe of the west side of Park Place across the street from the Zoo.

During that 7-block walk to the grocer, we'd pass Omicron Chi's house and there'd always be a small green MG two-door sports car parked on the main street. My grandmother would order us to make sure we purchased a 2-seater like that when we were old enough, so we'd have something of our own and didn't have to ferry around a crowd. That car became a metaphor and most of all an enduring subliminal message to strike out big and dream even bigger because we never had a car or a telephone in my grandmother's house the entire time I grew up. We did get a telephone in my senior year of high school for a few months and my grandmother maintained it to communicate with Reny and I when we went off to college.

Putting It All Together

There is certainly value in every lesson learned as a child. We must accept the fact that children's learning curve is influenced by every event until they learn to discern and distill the lessons through growth and understanding. In my case, my grandmother served as the teacher and provider to both my brother and I and to my mother who digested the lessons quite differently. Our journey and hers are markedly different and provide for interesting dialog that factor contrastingly and give proof to the value of learning from and processing instruction given from the same source. Momma as I'll refer to her is my grandmother, a wise no nonsense teacher who ruled with a velvet hand. She never once subscribed to the adage "spare the rod" as she doled out lessons with measured authority.

The "wake up" lesson lasts forever. It's easy to practice and establishes a baseline and starting point for one of leadership's governing tenants, discipline. Discipline was a key component to my upbringing, establishing rules and staying within the guidelines of those rules. We learned quickly because any violation resulted in an "unequal reaction." A perfect example of a childhood experience that crosses two lanes that I'll emphasize in personal synthesis of leadership, discipline, and restraint. One's ability to use solid judgement and resist temptation was grounded by a sound foundation in religion.

Once in the fourth grade, a young friend demonstrated a boomerang that he tossed during the entire lunch period on one memorable spring day. I was absolutely intrigued by the mechanics and played alongside him until recalled to class. He was a good companion and could always be trusted to be a solid friend in any situation and mind you we were on the cusp of integrating schools and this was only my second semester in an integrated school. John insisted that I take the boomerang home to play with overnight. After promising to return with it in the morning we exchanged salutations and went our separate ways. My peers took the bus home and he walked to a nearby neighborhood in the Lakewood section of my hometown in Norfolk.

I recall playing with the boomerang after dinner with my brother in momma's living room upstairs. Yes, we lived on the second floor of a one-family home in the Park Place section of town. My brother and I broke the quiet rule enforced in the evening hours and haphazardly whipped the toy around without regard for discretion. You see, momma had a long-standing rule about begging, borrowing, and stealing. We were to do neither or face the wrath of her strap without question or explanation. Our lack of discretion revealed a kink in the leadership armor that my grandmother was molding. We lacked the discipline to be quiet as instructed during the evening hours and I was found guilty of borrowing something even though my intent was to return it the next day. A clear violation of the restraint rule that leadership requires. A good leader is not impulsive nor should they demonstrate laxity at any time. The resulting impact was a "nod to the rod". As I grew older, my friends would steal bicycles and other toys from various locations and take them home without consequence. I would never do such a thing in my grandmother's house and the restraint and discipline learned through the simple and innocuous boomerang debacle lasts forever.

There were numerous examples of leadership tenants that my grandmother enforced without formally declaring lessons in life. They were simply applied, and lessons were cataloged easily as education became a way-forward. Integrity was the residual fallout of many lessons. Honesty was enforced in all situations. The problem with twins though is who owns the truth. My grandmother made that decision easy. She simply punished us both so declaring a side was not difficult and punishment proved to be always mitigatingly fair. We soon learned that honesty would reduce the distribution of punishment over time. Mistakes are inevitable and integrity proved to be a sure-fire way of making sure it was known to be only a mistake.

Poverty was a way of life in the neighborhoods we lived in after my stepfather departed. Glaring examples were a constant. Rundown secondhand property, rat infested hovels, dirty children's clothes and other outward signs reminded me of my unrequested plight. My grandmother however, lived by common sense rules and for the purposes of this chapter let's call it discretion. She always said nobody has to know you're poor. The lesson applied to this principle is often spoken in commonly expressed cliches like, "first impressions are the last impressions" or "never let 'em see you sweat."

We learned how to sew, clean, wash clothes, cook and maintain personal items at a very young age. Converse All Stars also known as Chuck Taylor sneakers were the only popular shoe at the time. The family's financial situation didn't allow for "flavor of the month" clothing accessories even though Chuck Taylor sneakers were a mainstay throughout American wardrobes and served as a fashion statement when color versions became popular. The first instantiations were basic black and white high top or low top shoes. Although my brother and I asked for these shoes constantly especially when we walked by the local Army Nave Store that featured the newest versions in its window display. My grandmother and mother for that matter resisted. We did get a fresh pair for the start of the school year but had to maintain them until the spring. Those shoes would inevitably wear thin at the sole and we'd resort to "shoe maintenance" and mitigated the hole by strategically placing cardboard or a precisely cut Parkay Margarine plastic top in the shoe. This worked well but was not a defense against winter so my grandmother did not allow us to wear sneakers during the winter until we became sophomores in high school.

In addition, she'd insist that we wash our sneakers routinely to make sure they looked presentable. Keeping them clean and fresh looking also required that we meticulously clean the rubber outer sole to eliminate scuff marks that a washing machines missed. Our shoes looked brand new all the time because we were not allowed to wear them if they appeared dirty, no matter the season. She enforced the same standard with clothing too. We had to iron our clothes at an early age. In addition, we had to polish the hard sole shoes we reluctantly wore in the winter or on rainy days because we simply could not wear sneakers when it rained, snowed or on any day that bad weather was forecast. This lesson of creating a clean appearance was a mitigating measure to making sure the world knew we were properly prepared and smartly dressed. Never understood the subliminal message of the "first impression." The mere fact that we had to be sharp at all times regardless of the cost or condition of clothing and shoes created a barrier to not only being looked down to as poor kids but being prepared in all first engagements.

Momma was simply a stickler for obedience and rule of law. Clothes were the outward appearance of our respectable self but cleanliness was the inward application of detail. We received marching orders about our stations for cleaning the house on a daily basis and the routine shifted with precision because she always remembered who completed the last task. Washing dishes and orderly room maintenance was a standard. Understand that we lived in two different locations with Ms. Bea. My mother moved us into my grandmother's house in the Ghent section of Norfolk in the late 1960's. We lived in that house for nearly 2 years. During that time we moved into my mother's newly rented apartment in another section of town called Villa Heights but life there was not ideal and we spent most of our time where we could reliably count on a meal, electricity, and warmth. My brother and I had to walk nearly eight miles when we couldn't get the proper nutrition needed. We'd simply walk from Villa Heights to West Ghent, the most run down tenement housing area in the city of Norfolk at the time. That's where we attended Robert E. Lee Elementary School, a segregated school in the center of ghetto life.

At Ms. Bea's house we learned order and organization. Each place was small and shoddy at best. In Ghent, we lived in a brownstone, lost relics to eventual gentrification that didn't take hold in Norfolk until the early 2000's. Five families lived in that single family brownstone. The families lived in "one roomers" on the main floors and one family lived in the attic my grandmother rented (sublet) to supplement our income. Each door to every room was locked with a pad lock because the owner didn't divide the place up through construction methods unlike our house in Park Place. There, the owner skillfully reengineered the house with two separate entrances and living spaces. The living space in the brownstone, however, did have separate kitchens but the quarters were open for all to travel ergo the need for padlocked doors. I mostly remember an odd feature of each door that was thankfully unique to the Ghent Brownstone. There were chewed out corners at the bottom of the doors near the kitchen which included the pantry and the dining room. Giant rats would eat through the wood and my grandmother resorted to using discarded can tops to patch them up on a routine basis as the rats never gave up on fighting to enter those areas. Fortunately she kept the food secure and safe and would throw away any container that appeared compromised. All in all the house in Ghent seemed bigger than the one we moved to in Park Place but things always appear bigger to the eyes of a child.

In either instance of the impoverished neighborhoods, we lived in, space was a premium, so order and organization was always key. I lived my later years from the late '60's to 1979 in Park Place on 32nd street on the second floor. The house no longer stands but the memories of the lessons learned there will live on forever. There were 3 rooms because it was a converted 2nd floor of a single-family house. The master bedroom, living room and dining room. There was a small kitchen and what now I understand to be a large walk-in closet that served as a second bedroom. Years ago, I looked at this condition as shameful and would not share these conditions but now I understand them to be building blocks for the character of the man I am to become. And the need for organization and order in such small spaces is essential. Another unique feature about both domiciles was the heating and air conditioning situation. My grandmother insisted on wood/coal burning stoves and refused to live in a house with central air and heat. It has taken years to understand the logic, but I've finally concluded that she didn't trust heating elements that she didn't control and therefore, she felt comfortable with these arrangements despite the times. It struck me that Momma only had one child of her own who died in a house fire at a very young age. I reason that she insisted on a wood/coal furnace because she always wanted to monitor the heater no matter the condition. The resulting outcome of this decision didn't bode well with my brother and I because we were embarrassed and forced to sleep in one room during winter until we grew up and appreciated our privacy. This was despite the chill in the winter and the number of blankets we used during cold winter nights. Call it character building but that's a lesson that only enforced my desire to own my own home and build it the way I wanted it to support my family. And we lived in this condition until I graduated from high school in 1979. I'm not embarrassed by this condition anymore because the lesson learned reinforces a desire to always be in control of my station in life.

Momma was a field general. Not only did she command respect, but she also earned it from those in her circle. She set an example for others and always lived her creed. A strict disciplinarian and shrewd family accountant. We never seemed poor and always had resources to get and do the things we wanted as kids. There was never a car in my life until I owned one as I explained. Knowing the bus schedule was a must and having the funds to ride it was an imperative because there simply were no other options. Walking and knowing the route was second nature. I entered the Army as an Infantry lieutenant and insisted on being a "straight leg" Airborne Ranger qualified grunt because I was no stranger to the "hum" as infantrymen called it. We walked and I was a seasoned walker who always knew the route. I was afraid of getting lost because a wrong turn in Ghent or Park Place could yield a fight from kids that didn't appreciate strangers on their block. It's strange now to think of this turf war that's fought on the streets of the ghetto because now I understand that nobody owned any property on either block. Although segregation did offer a twist this nearly 75% truthful fact.

One doesn't learn to appreciate their creed until they understand the value of that creed and how people honor their position in life. It is easy to say set the example but the code itself is easily compromised. It was Edgar A. Guest who pinned the poem "Live your Creed", a poem that I was forcefully introduced when pledging my fraternity in 1982 at Albany State College in Albany, Georgia. I learned later that Momma had a "Creed" and lived it every day. Not only did she talk the talk as often cliched by many, but she also walked the walk. Making sacrifices to make sure my mother, brother and I were provided for without ever showing the slightest angst or fatigue. She woke early to light the stove on cold days and turned on the oven in the kitchen to warm the back rooms before we rose for school. She made sure her appearance was always immaculate. Old clothes didn't look old on Momma. She ironed and pressed them daily and never compromised. She insisted that we do the same, but her example was what Guest referred to in his statement "the eye is a better pupil and more willing than the ear:" In sum, she set the example daily and insisted that we all looked presentable before leaving the house.

Living a "creed" of humility while trying to keep up with the times was harder than one can imagine during the times of afros, stack heeled shoes and braids. Momma never let us leave the house with plaits or braids in our hair no matter the style. And as the unfamiliar "do-rag" fad hit the scene in the late 1970's I carried on the policy and would never be caught dead outside with one on my head for fear that my grandmother's spirit would rise with the ROD. So, setting the example and putting on my best face and clothes is a standard and leadership trait that I carry today. Exempli Gratia!

Leadership requires that we make the sacrifices and be the example. General Norman Schwarzkoff said "the truth of the matter is that you always know the right thing to do. The hard part is doing it." I saw Momma sacrifice and live through the conditions without showing distress in any situation. She always displayed tolerance and humility. The times required humility but the tolerance was selective. As a leader, one must decide what battle to fight and what hilltop to die on if need be. Once that decision is made, they must demonstrate tenacity of purpose and resolve. Accepting the fate of subordinates through sacrifice, resilience and character is the sign of true leadership and I learned that through my grandmother's example.

Grit and courage are also key leadership traits although not phrased as such in leadership manuals. Momma was fearless. Again, she picked the battles and fought relentlessly to win no matter the cost. She was simply courageous beyond belief.

The ghetto is a scary place for anyone. Through the eyes of kids, it can be best described as simply confusion. Before a modicum of integration took hold, ghettos were unique. In segregated neighbors the majority class could be distinguished by identifiable characteristics. The rich lived in "wealthier looking" neighborhoods with properly manicured lawns surrounding stately expensive houses. The middle class lived in polished establishments adorned with lawns that were probably maintained by the family. The rich would more than likely hire someone or a service to maintain the estate but the hard-working middle class blue or white collar usually took pride in maintaining their own properties.

The poor neighborhoods for Black people included other ostracized minorities who suffered the indignation of oppression and prejudice including Hispanics who chose not to "pass" for white. This neighborhood (ghetto) was singular in dimension. There were few middle-or upper-class neighborhoods for blacks. The most distinguishing feature of the ghetto in the 1960s and 70's was the inclusion of all classes of Black people. Redlining, segregation and a threatening housing situation forced all classes of Blacks in a single location for the most part. Some owned houses but most rented during that period. A doctor could very well live next door to a janitor who shared yards with a single mother renting a 3 room hovel at an inflated price.

The housing available in those markets were usually houses abandoned by previous owners that exercised "white flight". This simply means that once a neighborhood opened to Black occupancy by law or financial opportunity, whites would put houses up for sale to flee that perceived surge of future black residents. The percentage that triggered white flight was about 1 percent in general. This meant that if a Black family moved into a property in a white neighborhood all the families would move almost immediately. This created enclaves of ghettos in the order of the city's allowance for Black movement. Owners would sometimes rent to the new occupants and sold to families who could afford a mortgage.

Renters would inflate the price and reconstruct houses to accommodate multiple families nearly doubling and tripling their monthly income. Housing was poorly maintained, and families compromised for the sake of living indoors. Landlords were notorious for providing shoddy maintenance and substandard fixes often using lead paints and asbestos (then legal) insulation. These compromised the health of occupants, but landlords proved to be systemically uncaring settling for profit and compromising safety.

A child living in these neighborhoods had no reference or vantage point to compare the situation with so a standard of compromise and inferiority was established early on. Schools suffered the same fate as well. Fortunately, Black teachers at the time provided first class lessons and guidance in a second-class facility using second and third-class tools and resources. With hindsight being 20/20, I now understand the value of this period as it applies to leadership. Humility is "a modest opinion of one's importance". It also defines the demeanor of one's character. A humble response controls the narrative and provides a projection platform to be respected. Aggressiveness in situations can be taken out of context even though it may be a simple outgrowth of confidence and surety. Humility is never mistaken and soothes the aggressor.

Momma always spoke of situational awareness from her perch in any situation. All people who live on the east coast or in major cities claim to be "faster". They swear by their ability to recognize trouble, opportunities, or challenges. Those from the deep south or from smaller cities are said to be "slow" and not really apt to catch on quickly. It can almost be considered a 6th sense of sorts in a hustle and bustle environment. Ms. Bea (as others called but Momma to us) was tenacious in making us astutely aware of our surroundings for safety purposes primarily. She essentially taught us how to judge a person's actions and behaviors and make quick and decisive engagements based on factors often overlooked by the naïve or uninformed.

To that end, I learned how to pay attention to everything including people, places, and things. People who didn't pay attention were easily victimized. Our house was always secure because we never let our guards down even though the 100 block of our neighborhood never fell victim to senseless crime. That fact, however, can be credited to all the neighbors who paid attention and passed on that very important skillset to all the children.

The most baffling value my grandmother applied was her belief in a strong education. She was born at the turn of the 20th century and completed high school in New York before moving in with her southern relatives in rural Yorktown, Virginia. Momma did not attend college. Norfolk State and Old Dominion University were well within reach but it was rare for a young Black woman in the early 1900's to attend college. Even though she did not attend she enforced the value of education and ruled study time with an iron fist. Never able to offer assistance, I can clearly remember her trying to answer questions based on her experience and basic temperament that expressed itself in such a manner as to give the illusion of having the answer to any complicated question.

She insisted that we complete our "lessons" or homework as it's commonly called. She didn't have the wherewithal to validate answers, but she knew that we had nothing else to do with the lights on and all electronics off from 4 PM till 7 PM on school nights. Nor were we allowed to venture outside during study hours. I find it difficult to reason why news reporters of today report on children dying during school days often midnight to five in the morning. We had a strict rule on school nights that required us to complete our "lessons" and play only until the streetlight came on in the neighborhood. We'd be ridiculed by our friends who were only allowed to stay out shortly after that and always before 9:00PM. That was simply a standing order for all and provided the backdrop for time to study and prepare for the next school day.

Ms. Bea would always insist that Reny and I attend college even though she didn't have any idea of how to prepare us financially, academically, or personally. The most unique thing about the education subject is my personal inability to remember anyone in my neighborhood who attended school at the university level. Momma drilled the concept in our heads because she was not keen on joining the military as a young person. Norfolk was full of military people and the road to success for an uneducated Black person was more than likely an enlistment to the military highway. Momma insisted that Reny and I were exceptional and didn't have to settle for enlisting in the service. And although we had no clue about how to prepare for college, her firm hand guided us along the way.

Momma became weaker and weaker as I grew older and stronger. She, however, always swore that she would never leave our sides until we were equipped to face the world alone. In 1979 I graduated from high school and matriculated to Marion Military Institute in Marion, Alabama. The road to Alabama was rocky because neither my brother nor I were prepared for a post-high school academic journey despite Ms. Bea's insistence. We simply never had the professional guidance to map a course to college. Fate, an astute Junior Reserve Officer's Training Corps (JROTC) Officer, and the grace of God was the fuel that covered the journey. While at Marion, Ms. Beatrice S. Harris rendered her final lessons.

Although we were poor, the trek to Marion provided the resources for the journey. A short trip to the Senior Army ROTC basic camp in Ft. Knox, Kentucky allowed Reny and I to compete for scholarships and also provided pocket money for the journey to Alabama later that summer. Momma made sure that we secured everything we needed for the journey and were prepared to provide a small stipend to help make ends meet. She showed us that even though she didn't know what it would take [that] she'd be financially prepared to support even if she had no details about the journey ahead. This proves to be a valuable lesson today. I know how to simply save for a rainy day and to be prepared to support when the opportunity presents itself.

We left for Marion the August and didn't return until Christmas because we both played on the schools Junior College Football team and played a junior college bowl game during Thanksgiving, my first away from home. When we arrived for Christmas, Ms. Bea looked weak and frail and finally started to show her 80 years of hard living. In a few days however, she perked up and became the "Momma" we always knew and loved. But one year later, Ms. Bea took her final breath and provided the final lesson with her departure. She skillfully left a gift of manhood to Reny and I. On February 14, 1981, Ms. Bea pinned us with responsibility and allowed us to grow knowing that she could no longer assist. She delivered on every promise till the day she died.

In conclusion, I've offered an assortment of lessons learned from my skillfully dedicated grandmother who grew up in an era where civil rights weren't a right. Her dutiful lessons live on and are surprisingly not unique to my household alone. As a middle aged, educated professional I continue to share these lessons with those less fortunate to have not been granted a living angel.

Chapter 11

PERSEVERANCE

DANNY COLEMAN

*But all the time
I'se been a'climbin' on,
And reachin' landin's,
And turnin' corners,
And sometimes goin' in the dark,
Where there ain't been no light.
So boy, don't you turn back;
Don't you sit down on the steps,
'Cause you finds it's kinder hard;*

I opened with this poem **Mother to Son** by Langston Hughes because it reflects one of the many lessons that my mother taught me.
My name is Danny D. Coleman and mother's name is Ernestine C.
Perkins. She is my source of inspiration and has provided many examples of perseverance. I also acknowledge other mothers who I've had the
pleasure of them inviting me into their homes and treating me like one
of their own, They include Amelia "Momma V" Vance, Ms. Ernestine
"Momma Cook", the mother of one of our close friends and teammates,
the late Fred Kennedy and Pauline Thomas, mother of our life-long
friend Ronald Haygood.

As I reflect on the many different stories and experiences that have shaped me into the man, father, son and provider I am today, there are too many to pen in the limits of my contribution to this book project. So, I will focus on a couple that really stand out and were instrumental to my growth into manhood. As a member of Omega Psi Fraternity, Incorporated, I learned as a young man, principles, faith and discipline would be my guiding light and establish my North Star. The Principles our founders agreed upon are Manhood, Scholarship, Perseverance and Uplift (Dreer 1940). This chapter shares personal stories and reflects on how I embraced the Perseverance principle, incorporated it into my personal and professional life and have done my best to use my mother and mother-like figures as examples to uphold my commitment to uplift the people and communities I serve daily.

As, I revisit the excerpt from the poem, I reflect on the parallel that my life has not been a "crystal stair". We all have to overcome obstacles, but how we approach and achieve success depends on the ability to not let life hold you back nor down. For as long as I can remember, my mother has had a strong work ethic. I've never seen one like it. She has always worked at least two jobs. Her perseverance has always led to her being a business of her own. Her businesses have included a paralegal service (Perkins Reprints) and a day care (Perkins Kiddie Kingdom). She has also served as a foster parent while even to this day worked a second job (she is 73 years young). My mother bought her house at age 25 and has maintained it ever since (with her children's love of course). This is special to me because she has done this as a single Black woman. Even though her race (black, white, or otherwise) should not matter, it does. She instilled an enduring work ethic in me since I was a child that lives with me as a man. I had a paper route at 10 years old and have continued to be gainfully employed since then.

I was blessed to have my mother as my boss at age sixteen. She also hired my friend and brother, Dr. Reginald E. Vance. Ironically, this was his first job in a corporate setting and greatly influenced his career path. The opportunity provided by my mother exposed both of us to the legal world. Our duties included making copies of transcripts and delivering them to attorneys in the Downtown Detroit business district. I was also able to use my talent as an artist to design flyers and other marketing materials for Perkins Reprints. I was able to refine my skills on the job and utilize them throughout my college career at Knoxville College in Tennessee. My mother encouraged us to make the most of the opportunity and experience of being around prominent professionals who we could learn various leadership attributes from and apply them wherever life took us. Dr. Vance (just Reg) at the time, took the job to another level. Whereas I was able to cultivate my artistic talent, Reg was absorbed into the environment of the attorneys and accountants in the office. He would read transcripts of cases and would love to sit and listen to trials as we waited for attorneys while they were deliberating cases. I never did take the job to that level. Watching the women in skirts was my extra-curricular activity (remember, I was only fifteen years old) with raging hormones that were on point. My mother made sure all those around her kept things in perspective while helping us establish priorities that would lead to our future successes. Momma P, as Reg calls her, never missed a chance to introduce us to men and women in those fine suits, fancy dresses, and shiny shoes.

There was one attorney that stood out-James B. Feaster. He was the step father of R&B singer Cherelle, one of Detroit's finest. He taught us two unintentional lessons. One, is that "a lot" of money is relative. I was tasked with making a lunch run. Feaster told me to look in the petty cash drawer and get some money for lunch. I looked in the drawer and made the mistake of saying out loud "Wow! This is a lot of money." Feaster lit into me hard. He looked at me with s stern grimace and said "A lot of money? – That ain't shit!" I was speechless, but I got it and the lesson has stayed with me. The amount of being "a lot" was relative to ones prosperity. Keep in mind I was merely fifteen years old and I was looking in the "petty cash drawer" of a distinguished, accomplished, and successful high power attorney.

The second lesson I recall is "get my name right". Reg and I actually overheard a phone conversation that Feaster was having. The party on the other end of the phone evidently kept mispronouncing his name. All Reg and I kept hearing was "Feaster like Easter man!" That person on the other end didn't say it correctly for several times. Then we heard him say "Feaster-Feaster as in Easter Man!" Reg and I were hysterically laughing our butts off. The lesson was get my name right. Still, until this day, I make it a point to make sure people pronounce my name right and spell it correctly. I make sure they call me Danny, not Daniel (that's my son's name). And, that my last name (Coleman) is spelled with an "e". Often, people spell it C-o-l-m-a-n. That doesn't fly with me because of the lesson I learned from Attorney James B. Feaster (rest in peace). My mother Ernestine Perkins introduced my friend, my brother to a whole new world that summer. A world that we were both able to successfully navigate with persistence and perseverance to accomplish what our mothers always believed we could. After all, each of our mothers were all of our mothers.

I went on to obtain a Master's degree and became a school teacher who has impacted the lives of thousands (students, mentees, parents, colleagues, superiors, and subordinates). Reg went on to obtain a Ph.D. and continues to work at the executive level in federal government and private industry. We both share a love for learning, teaching and leading. None of this is possible without mothers who instilled principles in us at an early age and held and continue to hold us accountable for being the best we can be in our churches, homes, schools, businesses, and communities.

Chapter 12

PROSPERITY

CHRISTOPHER PIRTLE
REGINALD E. VANCE

It has been simply amazing how this book project has brought authors and contributors together to share stories of how their mothers and mother-like figures influenced their leadership journeys. As I reviewed each chapter, it struck me that each contributor embodies similar leadership attributes, common aims and strong desires to help others while making the world a better place. In this final chapter, we share how motivation, optimism and momentum lead to prosperity. To do so, I asked my Fraternity Brother Christopher "Chris" Pirtle to join me in writing the culminating installment.

While the authors and contributors worked independently, their stories intertwine to weave a fabric that is timely, topical and enduring. According to Napoleon Hill's New Edition (2015) "No individual has sufficient experience education, native ability, and knowledge to insure the accumulation of a great fortune without the cooperation of other people." We agree. For several decades, Brother Pirtle has diligently applied his God given financial management consulting talents to enrich others. Like Danny Coleman in chapter eleven, Chris leads with a poem all Omega Men commit to memory and use as a source of strength throughout life to remind them of their mother and son life journey. Both share a motivation only mothers can provide. The motivation for a son to make his mother proud.

> *Well son, I'll tell you: Life for me ain't been no crystal stair. It's had tacks in it, And splinters, And boards torn up, And places with no carpet on the floor---Bare. But all the time, I'se been a-climbin' on, And reachin' landin's. And turin' corner. And sometimes going in the dark. Where there ain't been no light.*
>
> *So boy, don't you turn back. Don't you set down on the steps. 'Cause you find its' kinder hard. Don't you set down on the steps. Cause you finds it's kinder hard. Don't you fall now—For I'se still goin', honey I'se still climbin', And life for me ain't been no crystal stair.*
>
> Mother to Son by Langston Hughes 1922

Prosperity: a noun, the state of being successful usually by making a lot of money. {Merriam-Webster}

Stacy Janiak understands how women can be a catalyst leading to inclusive prosperity and writes "In a time when both businesses and society are searching for a return to growth and prosperity, I think we should understand that positive momentum works from the inside out. Growth-oriented leaders committed to creating a future built on a foundation of inclusion and equity should embrace the mindset of inclusive prosperity: prosperity that reaches far beyond the confines of business and ultimately drives greater societal impact." Janiak shares a sense of optimism we can all cling onto and share with others. We are better leaders once we understand strength in unity and that we have more in common than things that separate us.

The prosperity of the mother is preordained in biblical times as referenced in (Isa. 66:12) "For this is what the LORD says: "I will extend peace to her like a river, and the wealth of nations like a flooding stream; you will nurse and be carried on her arm and dandled on her knees."

The coin jar

While writing the final chapter of this book project, I shared with Brother Christopher Pirtle the story of the coin jar. For as long as I can remember, my mother, Momma V, maintained money jars to assure while we were economically disadvantaged, we were never broke or poor. My father Arron Vance, Sr. did the same. The basic concept is to take the coins out of your pockets at the end of the day and deposit them into receptacles of your choosing. We chose jars. If something unexpected happens, there is always a "go to stash". Most of my family members learned to do and continue to practice the same. Momma V would often lament "if you watch your pennies, the dollars will take care of themselves."

The money jars grew from simple mason jars to larger five gallon empty water bottles. Chris shared with me he has a five gallon water bottle that has been accumulating coins and dollars for more than twenty years. Great minds think alike. Thanks to Momma V and other mother-like figures, there was always money in the coin jars to protect us from unforeseen or impending dangers. Our mothers leave their legacy in such endearing subtle and genuine ways. Galford and Maruca (2006) posit "Legacy thinking is not a substitute, or synonym for a leader's organizational vison, mission and strategy." We believe our mothers had the foresight to instill a legacy of saving and being prepared for the unforeseen. It is much better to have and not need than to need and not have. Something as simple as consistently placing money in a coin jar over time can make all the difference in a leader's discipline and approach to setting examples for their organization, their followers, and their children who will lead future generations. Thanks MOM!

As we offer and share lessons of leadership in 2022 throughout this book project, I still have a coin jar with enough money to pay a major bill or respond to an unforeseen emergency. We believe our mothers and fathers learned this concept from the stories their ancestors shared with them about the Freedman's Savings and Trust Company which was chartered by the United States Congress in early 1865 for the benefit of ex-slaves and Black soldiers. Mothers around the world still use the coin jar or cookie jar methodology to save for rainy days. Prosperity starts at the basic level. As good stewards of legacy, it is incumbent upon us to follow our mother's lead and produce future leaders with a mindset of earning while saving and spending less than they earn. Channeling Ms. Bea, Brother Angelo Riddick says it best in Chapter Ten – Preparation. "Get up! Men don't lay around all day. Find something to do." This is truly a lost art in times of instant gratification. We understand and have empathy for mothers who are raising boys to be men without the aid of father figures. We also encourage all women to use their influence to make sure our next generation of men become just that-men with a healthy sense of responsibility, work ethic and pride. Get up! Don't lay around all day. Find something to do that increases the legacy your mother fought hard to establish.

Chris suggests mothers are the most fearless, resourceful and creative individuals walking the planet Earth. The most amazing of all God's creatures, a mother is truly a leader unlike any other. On her journey to prosperity, many different versions of motherly leadership traits appear. To most mothers, prosperity is not about how much money or wealth they have accumulated in life. It's about living a life worth living. It means providing for their children by any means necessary. A mother will go without in order to make sure their child has food every day, the finest of clothes and education opportunities. Mothers will themselves face hunger and many a sleepless night. All in the name of providing a meaningful life for their children. Prosperity to a mother is sitting back and watching her children run, smile and play under the sunlight, all the while her children not knowing what she had to sacrifice in order to the allow them the liberties most take for granted.

Mothers find a way. When all hope seems futile, they find a way. When rent is due and no check is to be found, a mother will find a way. When their child is hungry and the child support check didn't arrive, a mother finds a way. A mother's resourcefulness seems invulnerable to the various situations they are placed in throughout their lives. A common concept of a mother in some communities is the survivor, that mother who is working two to three jobs, a single mother struggling to put food on the table. The popular version of mothers we see in media today is that of the Housewife popularized by Bravo TV. Flaunting their perceived wealth, wining and dining with no visible source of income. This is the version of prosperity we want to believe, but is it real? Is it healthy? Is it reality?

No, the real prosperous mother is that queen who takes care of her family, her husband and then herself. That's the mother we worship for what she has given to her family, her children and her community. The queen. A mother who is grounded in the foundational and enduring aspects of prosperity. That mother understands her leadership examples shape the leadership journey of her children and others. She is grounded in teaching, nurturing and giving more of her self-prosperity than commonly capable of other women or men. If you seek to gain a better understanding of prosperity, we recommend you look deep into the examples of sacrifice your mothers and mother-like figures you have exhibited throughout life.

We encourage all readers and receivers of the messages, stories and examples contained in this book to live in the prosperity our mothers slaved for, fought for, marched for and died for in order that we could live the dreams and visions of the prosperity all mothers want for their children.

CONCLUSION

Our goal for this book project was to look at leadership from the perspective of what mothers do in order to assure the success of their children and others in their communities. It started out as a series of poems my mother and I wrote to each other and loved ones. We shared those poems as sources of inspiration while we dealt with my mother's colon cancer battle. The project evolved into what is sure to be a seminal manuscript for anyone interested in celebrating mothers' ability to groom and grow effective leaders. We hope this compendium of leadership journey stories about how mothers and mother-like figures shape the lives of others becomes a must read for anyone pursuing a leadership path or wanting to understand what is required to be an effective leader.

I have been asked over the years "how are you able to operate at such a high energy level and help so many people without burning yourself out?" My answer is that my life's mission is to follow the examples of my mother and help as many people as I possibly can. After all, that is what true leadership is all about. Creating the vision and mission as well as helping people achieve their goals while inspiring them to help others.

Why do I lead? When do I lead? Where do I lead? We believe, the answers to those questions, more often than not, are found in the wisdom and actions of our mothers. People say the love of a mother is the greatest gift one can ever hope to experience. Each contributor to this book shared their admiration of their mother and her leadership style as the foundation of their leadership journey. These benchmarks and milestones of peaceful and productive living guide us through the most complex situations we face in life. They prepare us to lead.

It is my most sincere hope that this book provides you and those around you with examples of the core principles required to be effective leaders in your homes, families, communities, churches, and organizations. We pray each reader has gained value in the lessons we shared throughout the book. We hope the lessons helped you in some small way. We hope you have found this book enlightening and worthy of sharing with others.

Be blessed and continue to be the leaders your mothers intended you to be.

TESTIMONIALS

"Now faith is the substance of things hoped
for, the evidence of things not seen"
-Hebrews 11:1

The power of a mother's faith is unmatched. Her influence on her children is beyond her imagination. Her faith creates the vision she carries for the future of her children.

A mother's faith is two-fold. One, she believes in the word of God, and that He will fulfill his promises. Second, she believes in her children, and that they can achieve anything they put their minds to.

A mother is charged with the responsibility for bringing life into the world and equipping her children with tools that create the character for a strong independent adult. She loves when we can't love ourselves. She believes when our confidence is low. She covers us when we have no clue to call on God

I am blessed that throughout my life I've had the honor of interacting with many mothers, or mother figures I consider spiritually inclined, or as we referred to while growing up "filled with the Holy Spirit." I would like to say thank you to not only my mother and those I've interacted with, but also to mothers and mother figures that have interceded on the behalf of the contributors and readers of this book.

From the inception, my mother Julette Dachelle Jones had the strength to raise nine children through the P.O.W.E.R of her faith. When I say P.O.W.E.R the acronym stand for Prayer, Optimism, Wisdom, Empowerment, and Resourcefulness.

Prayer was intentional and consistent in our household. My mother taught us to pray before eating, traveling, making decisions, big endeavors, going to bed and for the well-being of all human beings. She would always say "allow God to do his part". My mother taught us that prayer opens communication and builds a partnership with God. She was big on us understanding that prayer was an act of faith. Through prayer we seek God's guidance, asked for what was needed, we praised and thanked Him for all His love, grace, and mercy.

My mother was a praying woman. She knew her duty was to take her children before God and plead for His blessings and guidance throughout their lives. The task of being a mother of nine was not easy. However, my mother was charged with it and did her best each day. Her prayer life and faith in God allowed her to optimistically look forward.

Optimism in a mother is having faith that all your needs will be fulfilled. No matter how challenging life became my mother was able to extract the positive aspects of any situation. Her optimistic outlook on life set the tone for her children to feel positive about overcoming any challenge that occurred. We were always able to sense when things weren't right, or plans didn't go as she thought, but she never showed defeat. She would bounce back quickly. This one quality she possessed greatly impacted all her children. She modeled taking on challenges with a positive outlook, expecting a positive outcome.

My mother was the epitome of optimism. She knew that her responsibility was to teach her children to control their emotions. She led by example. She used every opportunity to take on life with a logical and expectant manner. My mother understood that having faith required an optimistic attitude to get through the process and to the end of whatever circumstance that was at hand. Throughout her life, her compass was using wisdom from her own or other experiences.

Wisdom is having the ability to apply your experience and knowledge for the soundness of actions and decision making. Today, I can recall so many times that my mother's advice was correct and I did what I desired. Even though, I would choose the opposite of what she suggested, I wouldn't be the woman I am today if it were not for my mother. Her wisdom imparted on my life was sound advice from experience. She would often say "there's nothing new under the sun." As an adult and a mother, I share the same sentiments.

My mother shared pearls of life as a woman and a mother with her children. She used wisdom to rear us into God-fearing, courageous, fearless individuals. Two of her sayings she'd use to empower us was "as long as you are alive time will pass, you may as well fulfill your desires" and "success is on the other side of fear." Each day these words still live strongly in my heart and are used as decision making factors. Empowerment and encouragement start in the home. A child learns who they are and their limitations far before entering the world. A mother of nine children experienced many challenges and was defeated by some. It's hard to imagine fighting your own battles and at the same time building confident children.

The words my mother use when communicating with us was powerful and intentional to build us up. She used positive affirmations to instill in us that we can do anything we put our minds to and we can overcome any obstacles. She created a safe place for us to release when we felt overwhelmed and ready to give up. She would give us a thirty second fit phase to appropriately address the emotions at moment. After that, she taught us how to cope, then to pray and trust that God will handle it. Her method of empowering was truly faith-based. She trusted God and used actions and resources to equip her children for success.

Resourcefulness for a mother is second nature. A mother must find ways to get things done. Children spark the creative mind of their mothers, which allows her to find ways to keep the household afloat. Sometimes having multiple solutions to single problems. I would often hear my mother say, "if there's a will there's a way." Not only did she say it, but she was also able to find a way for us to enjoy a simple life. She made a way to ensure we had the necessities that allowed us to adjust to the universe around us. She taught us to have a resourceful mindset. To think outside of the box, be creative, and visualize all possible ways to achieve a positive outcome. In that, we learned not to be quitters and to try new ways and options. "If there is a will, there is a way."

Julette Dachelle Jones prided herself on leading our home through the P.O.W.E.R. of faith. She raised nine courageous children and taught them to live and thrive by having faith. She role modeled strength of steel and did her best to provide stability emotionally, mentally, physically, and spiritually for us. We learned to live in partnership with God through faith. The teachings from my mother on prayer, optimism, wisdom, empowerment, and resourcefulness is used daily to guide decision making and provide guidance in our lives.

Cherron Jones

Yes, Mr. Mayor, I will fulfill your request. The Godly Leadership of a Godly Mother

I called the Mayor of the District of Columbia; he was in a meeting and he requested me to text him. Alarmingly and equally concerning for me, I asked myself, "What is a text"? It was at that exact moment, I realized I had never heard of this brand of modern communication! However, as the Mayor's Transition Religious Chairperson, I remembered hearing my Mother, Pastor Katie's words of strength. "Always operate with the strong hand, never demonstrate weakness, pray, pause, ask, research, gather all pertinent information, continuing to perform your life's homework with excellence in each and everything you do, finding a way to always present yourself to be strong and continue your Prayers to God." I was reminded in those very few seconds of the teachings and leadership of my Pastor, who is my Mother, before I ended the phone call. I said with a certainty to the Mayor of the District of Columbia, "Yes, Mr. Mayor, I will fulfill your request and text you."

Now between you and I, as I was driving down the street where the United States Capitol sits, I had not a clue, how to make this work, but I knew from witnessing my Mother's indomitable strength, as a little boy growing up in Mississippi, that failure was not an option and I only had minutes to 'text' the awaiting Mayor. It's at that point that I began to pray with my eyes wide open and had a talk with God, as I have so often seen my Mother who is my Pastor do, and behold, there emerged to my vision, bright lights illuminating from a prominent Church having Choir Rehearsal. Being familiar with this Church and Pastor Rev. Dr. Lewis Anthony, I quickly parked the car, walked hurriedly to the entrance of the Church, opened the doors, found Pastor Anthony, conveyed my dilemma, he then begin showing me how to text as he himself had recently learned and I then sent the Mayor the text with the information requested. The spirit of determination that led me to that church that day is directly attributed to lessons my mother taught and showed me time after time. After serving and assisting 5 United States Presidents both Democrats and Republicans, 5 District of Columbia Mayors, first Clergy to be officially trained by Members of the US Congress in a special Congressional Political, Educational and Leadership Training Institute, organizing, coordinating thousands upon thousands of local, national and world leaders and a now Two-Time Recipient of the President of the United States' "President's Lifetime Achievement Award" by both President Joseph R. Biden and President Barack H. Obama, I can un-equivocally without hesitation, say that none of this would have been made possible, if it was not for God, Christ Jesus and my Extremely Strong Leader, Role Model and Virtuous Mother, Pastor Katie R. Foster Anthony.

At my Mother's home going celebration of life service, as a result of her values, ambition, resilience and wise leadership, leaders from around the nation and world sent official letters and words of expression i.e., US Congresspersons, US Ambassadors, her fellow Ministerial Colleagues Reverend Jesse L. Jackson and Reverend Al Sharpton, Chairperson Emeritus of the NAACP, the Mayors of Gulfport, Biloxi and Washington, DC, the National Director of the Smithsonian Institution National Museum of African American History and Culture, the National Presidents of the National Bankers Association, the US Black Chambers Incorporated, the National Association of the Black Hotels, Owners, Operators and Developers, the American Federation of Government Employees (AFGE) and as a proud member of Omega Psi Phi Fraternity Inc., my Sorority Sister, my Mother, Pastor Katie R. Foster Anthony, a lifetime member, received special greetings from the past National President of Delta Sigma Theta Sorority, Inc., Reverend Dr. Gwendolyn Boyd.

In summation, I find myself in countless scenarios as mentioned above and my Godly Mother's words of wisdom, is what continues to propel me and others, as we strive daily to follow the footprints of her Godly Leadership.

Reverend. Dr. George E. Holmes

While pledging the greatest fraternity on earth, Omega Psi Phi Fraternity Inc., I was privileged to be introduced to a poem written by Brother Langston Hughes, titled "Mother To Son". There is a line in this poem that says, "Life for me ain't been no crystal stair." Over the course of my life, I watched my mother, Ima Jean Simpson, sacrifice her own financial gains, unselfishly forfeit objects of desire, minimize her own personal needs, and relinquish to her family and children her position as center of her universe. My mother surrendered her opportunity for that metaphoric crystal stair to provide me the resources to elevate myself educationally and personally. Her discipline, guidance and direction taught me to be a good person, a man of integrity, and a loving father. "Treat people how you want to be treated in return", is the advice she gave me as a child, and I have carried that with me throughout my life. I was privileged enough to come from a traditionally structured family but was unfortunately unable to have that structure sustained throughout due to circumstances well beyond my control. But my mother held steadfast and never wavered in her mission to instill in my brother's and me the importance of not only being a good person but in being a great man. Life is unfair sometimes, which I am unfortunately having to face currently with my mother's fatal illness but leaning on my own understandings would defy my trust in God, so I acknowledge him, allow him to direct my path, and know that I am grateful and so very thankful for the mother I was blessed with. I'm heartbroken knowing the inevitable, but I'm overjoyed and full of warmth from all the loving memories I will cherish forever. This woman is my hero in all sense of the word. So Ma, I'm not going to turn back, or set down on the steps, because it's so very hard, but nor will I fall, because you have instilled in me the will to hold on and continue to climb. THANKYOU MY LOVE.

Christopher Simpson

Leaders are usually Type A personalities; some are born that way and others are developed over time. We are outgoing, ambitious, rigidly organized, impatient, proactive, and concerned with time management. I do not consider myself highly status-conscious or anxious which further describes Type A folks. As an entrepreneur in the medical field, leadership is paramount or you suffer consequences. It includes leading by example, working long and tough hours. It also requires sacrificing some wants for needs until the company is in a better position. I often think about my mother's journey as the eldest child from the suburbs of Cleveland, Ohio to becoming a Principal of Coffee Middle School in Detroit. She is a Classic Type A personality and I guess this apple didn't fall far from her tree. She worked long hours helping students get ahead while still remaining active in the community. Women in large corporations are often subject to sexism and the Detroit Public School system was no different, especially in the 70's and 80's. Women weren't considered outright Principal material but she proved them wrong at every turn. She never brought home what she was dealing with at work, she was able to drop that stress at the door and pick it back up the next day. My mom was able to raise two boys in the inner city of Detroit without immediate family around to support her. We didn't have much as educators are paid a fraction of their worth but made due with what was there. She taught me firsthand what a leader looked like.

Dr. James Anderson

When it comes to the strength and leadership of a woman, Proverbs 31:28-31 reminds me of my mother, Ms. Purline Bryant.

Proverbs 31:29 stands out for me, because my mother raised six daughters, all virtuously.

My mother is blessed to be 80 years old, still sound-minded and all six of her daughters are still alive, there's Marie, Lisa, twins, Linda and Brenda, Teresa and Regina, now that's a blessing in itself. She is also blessed to be a grandmother and a great-grandmother.

My mom would awake early morning to prepare breakfast and lunch for my dad before he left to open his Mobil gas station. She would then get us girls washed and dressed and then prepare a hot breakfast for each of us (there weren't any microwave ovens, nor boxed cereal) pancakes from scratch. While we were at school she was not sleeping, she was a seamstress and sewing all our clothes and some for our neighbors.

After school she helped us with our homework, fed us a hot dinner then got us ready for bed. She was the first one awake and the last to close her eyes, just to do it all over again. My mom showed up for everything.

She is well known to be a seamstress, cook, Bible Study teacher, community activist, and chauffeur to name a few hats

My mother returned to college after leaving my dad with her six daughters to obtain her undergraduate and master's degrees as a licensed social worker. All six daughters are college-educated women too, Marie has a bachelor's in communications, Lisa has a bachelor's in business administration and human resources, Linda bachelors in business administration. Brenda master's in nursing, Teresa masters a degree in psychology, and Regina has a double masters in science and biology.

My mother's legacy continues with her grandchildren being college educated as well. One of her grandsons has his doctorate, a granddaughter with a master's degree, and several with a bachelor's degree.

Hats off to my mom, Ms. Pearl

Lisa Cowan

I was born on August 12, 1959. My mother and father were both born to families of sharecroppers growing up. This story will help you understand my mother's influence on my development of leadership qualities. My mother's maiden name was Lillian Malveaux and she was from Opelousas, Louisiana. During her upbringing in grade school, she reminded me and my brother, John Anthony Charles, that her brothers and sister were sharecroppers in grade school. They worked the fields often picking cotton, during harvest before they went to school. Her parents would wake them up at 5am to work the fields before going to school to get an education. My mother did not like the fact that her brothers were drafted at a young age, to serve, in the armed forces, to serve, during the Korean and Vietnam Wars. Her parents died at a young age which meant as the elder daughter, she had to cook and clean for her seven brothers and sister. She played basketball in high school and was a shooting guard.

My mother met my father, Louis Charles, and moved to Houston, Texas where I was born and raised. Growing up, my mother was a strict disciplinarian. She attended Texas Southern University and received a bachelor's degree in Education with a focus in Special Education. While going to school, she made sure we were prepared to go to school in the morning. Upon completion of her degree, she started a career in education in the school systems in and around Houston. She emphasized the importance of believing in God, going to church, and staying prayed up. She also emphasized the importance of education in the church as my mother and father were raised in the catholic church. My mother's influence on me in leadership came as she was a visionary and always lead by example.

She had a vision of me playing the saxophone in grade school. She was at every performance when not working and supported all band fundraising efforts. In my junior year in high school, she served as a chaperone when our jazz band toured Hawaii. In my senior year, where I was offered many music scholarships, she encouraged me to try engineering as I made good grades in mathematics and thought I would have a better career in engineering. I had two opportunities in engineering at Prairie View A&M University and Southern University. I chose Prairie View A&M University because it was closer to home and I wasn't sure I would like to be away from home. I would learn early on that I had to study to make the grades at Prairie View.

Once I became a member of Rho Theta Chapter, Omega Psi Phi Fraternity, Incorporated, and was elected Keeper of Records & Seal, I had to balance studying and socializing. I briefly lost my merit scholarship and turned to my mother for support. She informed me that she would help me one time then I would have to apply myself as she didn't send me to college to party. I enrolled in Advanced ROTC and made the honor roll my last five semesters. When I graduated with honors and was commissioned a Second Lieutenant in the United States Army, my mother and father were present. My mom was present at every promotion thru Major, graduation from the Signal Officer Advance Course, and visited every duty station except Seoul, Korea. She made sure I knew she didn't approve of me being on active duty due to her experience of losing her brothers to the draft and war. When I retired from the Army as Lieutenant Colonel, she wanted to attend to make sure this chapter was closed.

My mother influenced my development in leadership as a visionary and leading by example. She was a strict disciplinarian who believed in the catholic church and God. My mother also believed that to be an effective leader, I must know my business and be knowledgeable of my subject matter. She wanted a better life for me than her upbringing.

Thanks MOM!

Sherman Charles

The very first time my mother Patricia Ann Gaddy put her trust in me as a young leader was at age 4. We would visit my Grandparents in Lumberton, North Carolina during the summer time. While there in Lumberton, Momma would take me to the store about a one-fourth mile up the road with her and introduce me to Ms. Emma, the store owner. Momma was planting a seed in me to be confident that I could walk to the store alone without her and buy her Items. That was a powerful lesson for me to learn that I can do things without my Momma leading the way, Momma's favorite Quote to me about Mr. WaterMan " It's All In Divine Order"

Taft Gaddy

My Inspiration, my Motivator, my go to, my Momma, my Everything-Dr Gaylene Perrault. Knowing what my Mother has been through in life and that what she made of herself taught me that as long as you NEVER GIVE UP good things will happen. I was born in New Haven, Connecticut and at that time my Momma was not very educated. She would walk pass Yale University often and then became an instructor there. With her hard work and NEVER GIVE UP attitude, she eventually got her Ph.D. from Michigan State University. I have never seen a person so determined and work so hard. While working hard to attain her education, she would fix wonderful meals and bake upside down pound cakes and invite me into her kitchen. The great Dr. Gaylene Perrault traveled the world, became an Instructor at the Spelman/Clark Atlanta University (AU) center. She raised three men and a daughter. Two of her children earned P.D.s, one is an entrepreneur one is a Chef who Caters to the Stars. NEVER GIVE UP thanks Momma. GOD is good!

Brett Smith

On behalf of the Miles's, I am beyond honored to share the impact of Momma Miles. Our mother, Mrs. Willie Alma (Robertson) Miles was a 4'11 dynamo, who spoke softly, but profoundly. She did not carry a *big stick* because her weapon of choice was kindness. She always had a smile on her face and kind a word for everyone who was blessed to be in her presence, whether deserving or not. Momma had a way of bringing the best out of the worst situations. She was the mother that miraculously made a dollar out of fifteen cents, every Christmas the merriest, every birthday special and the tooth fairy real! As a mother of five (Deirdra,Tamra, Edward, Valachie, Jeannie) very distinct personalities and an Educator in the Louisiana Public School System for over forty years, she impacted the lives of generations and generations to come. After a long, hard fought battle, during the COVID-19 era, we lost our mother to dementia on July 27, 2020. As I sit here on Mother's Day, May 8, 2022 missing her like crazy, I lean to the comfort of the most profound lesson she ever taught... Read on!

"This too shall pass". Mama always prefaced her following words of wisdom with this cliché. Anytime we thought we were plagued with impending doom, without the strength to go on...*yet again*... and had come to seek wise counsel at the foot of the ALL KNOWING (mama) she would just remind us in her calmest voice that this too shall pass and that trouble does not last always. Her next question would always be, *Have you prayed about it?* As a child or young adult even, this was not always the answer we wanted from THE PERSON WHO SOLVED ALL PROBLEMS. We may not have realized it at that moment, but Mama was equipping us (and countless other) with the necessary tools to get through any situation; PERSERVERANCE AND PRAYER. Armed with the peace of knowing that anything is possible and a prayer life that sustains us through it all was the best examples of a Mother's Love and Leadership we could have asked for. Thank you Mama!

Jeannie Miles-Essone

POEMS

Ain't I A Woman?
By Sojourner Truth

Well, children, where there is so much racket there must be something out of kilter. I think that 'twixt the negroes of the South and the women at the North, all talking about rights, the white men will be in a fix pretty soon. But what's all this here talking about?

That man over there says that women need to be helped into carriages, and lifted over ditches, and to have the best place everywhere. Nobody ever helps me into carriages, or over mud-puddles, or gives me any best place! And ain't I a woman? Look at me! Look at my arm! I have ploughed and planted, and gathered into barns, and no man could head me! And ain't I a woman? I could work as much and eat as much as a man - when I could get it - and bear the lash as well! And ain't I a woman? I have borne thirteen children, and seen most all sold off to slavery, and when I cried out with my mother's grief, none but Jesus heard me! And ain't I a woman?

Then they talk about this thing in the head; what's this they call it? [member of audience whispers, "intellect"] That's it, honey. What's that got to do with women's rights or negroes' rights? If my cup won't hold but a pint, and yours holds a quart, wouldn't you be mean not to let me have my little half measure full?

Then that little man in black there, he says women can't have as much rights as men, 'cause Christ wasn't a woman! Where did your Christ come from? Where did your Christ come from? From God and a woman! Man had nothing to do with Him.

If the first woman God ever made was strong enough to turn the world upside down all alone, these women together ought to be able to turn it back and get it right side up again! And now they is asking to do it, the men better let them.

A Mother's Love

By Amelia J. Vance

Admired, cherished, and loved so much
Giving, caring, sharing her love all the time
Nothing that I know is like a Mother's touch
Nothing can compare to the dear sweet mother of mine

She was always there with good advice to share
Never once was my call to her denied\
A mother's love will always show you that she cares
Even late in the midnight hour, my mother's love I have tried

Sometimes unnoticed she may have seemed to be
The thoughts of her smile, so much happiness they bring
I remember mother, and to her sweet memories I will cling and obey
Because my mother's love was truly the wind beneath my wings

God gave us only one mother to love, cherish and obey
We should love her, because, like her there is no other
So lift up your mother and love her each and every day
There is nothing on this earth that can ever take the place of a mother

Remember your mother's love when thoughts of her come your way
Remember the good times you shared with her and smile
Remember her love for Christ and how she lived for God each day
Remember your mother's blessings because she was truly God's child

The love of a mother can never be told
The love of a mother will never die
The love of a mother is worth more than silver and gold
The love of a mother will reach beyond the sky

The love of a mother is so very true
Holdfast to and do not forsake your mother's love
The love of your mother will always be there for you
Because the love of a mother is God sent from above

All My Children

By Amelia J. Vance

———

The proud Mother of ten living children
I love you all so dearly

So, to all my children, to me you are the Bold and the Beautiful
To say the least

Even though things seem bleak sometimes, you
must pursue your utmost dreams
And, when you encounter Dark Shadows

As you venture through life, remember the teaching you received
from your mother when you were Young and Restless

Keep your focus on the Lord and this will be your Guiding Light
Your Search for Tomorrow will not be smooth sailing

But if you believe in yourself you will find that as the World Turns,
Your hopes and dreams will all come true as long as you don't give up
and don't become weary because you only have One Life to Live

And you must live it to the fullest

You must love each other and stick together through all our generations
Together we can be strong and powerful all the Days of Our Lives

Remember divided we can only build a hut but
together we can build a Dynasty
So take on the challenges that you face

Move the largest mountain. Dream the impossible dream.
Fight he unbeatable fight. Right the unrightable wrongs.

Be strong

You can do it. Nothing is impossible for you because you are
All My Children

My Strong Black Mother

By Reginald E. Vance, Ph.D.

———

Her skin is as smooth as silk. Not a worry line will you find.
On her own, a house of love she built. And to the problems of life, I was blind.

There was never quite enough to eat or fancy clothes to wear.
But, somehow all the burdens of the world she would bear.

She's my Strong Black Mother. And I love her.

I am the youngest of ten. We were all taught and loved the same.
We stumble and falter every now and then. But,
she's always willing to take the blame.

We are her babies each and every one of us.
Through the toughest of times, I never once heard her fuss.

As amazing as it may be and as impossible as seems,
She makes it possible for me to keep sight of my dreams.

I thank God for my Strong Black Mother. And I love her.

A goddess of love; she's always been my mother and my father.
The things she's done, I'll always remember.

Sent from heaven above; caring for all of us is never a bother.
Her love keeps us warm in the coldest of December.

Seasons change.

But, her devotion to twenty needing eyes never fades.

Battle after battle! I have lost count of her endless love crusades.

When tears and torment are too much to bear,
She spreads her wings of love and showers us with prayer.

She's my Strong Black Mother. And I love her.

Certain things I reason. Others I can't understand.
Too beautiful of a creation; she's more than a mere woman.

Try to imagine raising five boys and five girls.
Now imagine piecing together ten shattered worlds.

She never has to imagine or play games of the mind.
If you look into her unselfish past, that's what you'll find.

A friend, a confidant, a reason to love is what she'll always be.

Oh' thank God for my Strong Black Mother and what she means to me.

Young Gifted and Black

BY AMELIA J. VANCE

———

Young Gifted and Black… The title I give to you
You are determined to complete what you set out to do

You were determined not to get lost or go astray
You struggled through some bad times but you found your way

Growing up was not easy being the youngest of ten but
you always knew the hardest battle you could win
Watching you grow up was a great joy because
I knew then I had a gifted Baby Boy

Like the little eagle, your will soars to the greatest heights
You will reach your destiny regardless of the flight

You made good decisions in life and followed them through
Venturing off sometimes, knowing I was there for you

Sometimes undecided but that's a part of life
God always helped you through the pain and strife

When you received your Bachelor's, your mind was not at rest
You then went for your Master's and achieved that major task

Why settle for so little, you thought within your mind
I'll get my PhD while I'm young and still have time

I have never doubted the extent of your ability
You are my son, and you can be anything you want to be

My love is always with you, in everything you set out to do
I know you will never give up; I have that faith in you

To accomplish your goals with your inner self you must stay on track
This I know you will do, because you are my son, Young Gifted and Black

My Momma Didn't Raise No Quitters!
By Reginald E. Vance, Ph.D.

———

I quit. I give up. I can't take anymore.
These are words planted in my mind that I have to ignore.

Things will never change. The dream is dead.
I battle each day to flush these thoughts from my head.

You are inferior. Your dreams won't ever come true.
I dispel those myths with everything I do.

You come from a dark continent. You have a dark past.
I hear these words and throw them out like trash.

You are a second class citizen. You should be treated like one.
I reflect on inhumane acts, and by whom they are done.

We owe you nothing. You should be happy to be here.
Each one of those lies paints a picture clear.

The young black race is destroyed. You're void of responsibility.
These blatant untruths encourage my creativity.

Your race is lazy. You're shiftless. All you want is welfare.
Statistics show for each of us in line, seven of them are there.

It's reverse discrimination and unfair education assistance.
The past thefts refute any manufactured evidence.

ABOUT THE AUTHOR

Dr. Reginald Eric Vance (Reggie Vance) was born in Brinkley Arkansas June 6, 1965, to Amelia and Arron Vance, Sr. When he was thirty days old, his mother moved the family to Detroit, Michigan where he matriculated through the Detroit Public School System (DPS), attending Kennedy Elementary School, Pelham Middle School, Cass Technical High School and Redford High School. Inspired early in life by the leadership examples of his mother Ms. Amelia "Momma V" Vance and other mother-like figures, Reggie accepted leadership roles early in life as an Alter Boy in the Church of Christ, Student Council at Kennedy Elementary School, Student Council, Trumpet Section Leader and Co-Captain of the Pelham Middle School two-time National Mathematics championship team, Co-Captain of the Redford High School Junior Varsity Basketball Team and Co-Captain of the Redford High School Baseball Team. He was born, bred and built to lead with a visionary mindset, heart of compassion and sense of accomplishment through excellence. He got that from his Momma!

After graduating from Redford High School in 1983, Reggie enrolled at Southern University and A&M College in Baton Rouge, Louisiana, where he continued his leadership journey in academics receiving acceptance in the Honors College Program his freshman year, student government leadership, community service organizations and athletics. He became a college professor at age 22, while completing his Master's degree in Mass Communications. Reggie benefitted from the love, nurture and guidance of mothers in Baton Rouge who became his surrogate mothers on campus, in churches he attended and the communities he served. They encouraged him to stay focused and work hard. They also encouraged Reggie to read and write with a compulsive passion. Their encouragement paid off. Dr. Vance has contributed to four other published books (The Black Male in White America (2002), African-Americans and Political Participation (2003), The History of Omega Psi Phi Fraternity, Inc.: An Update for the Period 1960-2008 (2009) and Uplift: Spiritual Uplift through Prayer, Sermons and Inspirational Scriptures (2021).

For the past 22 years, Vance has served in several senior level leadership positions with the federal government, government affinity organizations, and civic organizations. In 2021, Dr. Vance negotiated the first ever Intergovernmental Personnel Act (IPA) agreement between the federal government and the City of Annapolis, Maryland. He assumed the role of Senior Executive Advisor to the City of Annapolis, Maryland where he provides consulting services to various management, program, and project teams. He studies the organizational goals, strategies, and business plans to determine what changes and process improvements are implemented to better serve the city's executive team and the people they serve. This includes facilitating an effective means for the City of Annapolis to develop, implement, and manage processes that improve administration of federal grants, policies, and programs. He reaches people and teaches leadership at all levels.

REFERENCES AND RESOURCES FOR FURTHER READING

Bacon, Terry R.. (2006). *What People Want*:
Mountainview, CA: Davis-Black Publishing.

Buford, Valerie. (2021) *Perseverance Helps You Survive in Tough Times*:
Palatine, IL: Book Vine Press.

Covey, Stephen. (2004). *The 7 Habits of Highly Effective People*:
New York, NY: Free Press.

Gates, Bill (2020)
U.S. Chamber of Commerce
Top Bill Gates Business Quotes (uschamber.com)

Gibran, Khahlil (2022). The Prophet:
White Plains, NY. Peter Pauper Press, Inc.

Harrell, Dwain (2021). *Uplift: Spiritual Uplift Through Prayer, Sermons and Inspirational Scriptures.*

Hill, Napoleon (2015) *Think and Grow Rich*:
New York, NY: Quarto Publishing Group USA Inc.

Jackson, Michael J. (2009). *Prostate Cancer: My Personal Journey.*

Janiak, Stacy
https://fastcompany.com/90701556/how-leaders-can-drive-growth-by-embracing-inclusive-prosperity

Jennings, Kenneth R. (2001). *The Serving Leader:*
Oakland, CA: Barrett-Koethler

Levine, Margie (2001). *Surviving Cancer.*
New York, NY: Random House, Inc.

Lencioni, Patrick (2002). *The Five Dysfunctions of a Team.*
San Francisco, CA: Josey Bass

Oakley, Ed and Krug, Doug (1991). *Enlightened Leadership.*
New York, NY: Fireside

Odom, Guy, R. (1989). Mothers, Leadership and Success.
Houston, TX: Polybius Press.

Robbins, Harvey and Finley, Michael. (2004). *The Accidental Leader.*
San Francisco, CA: Josey-Bass.

Toller, Lynn (2007). My Mother's Rule
Chicago, IL.

Vann, Paul Lawrence (2005). Living on Higher Ground
New York, NY: Laurel Wreath Publishing

White, B. Joseph (2007). *The Nature of Leadership.*
USA

Woolfe, Lorin (2002). *Leadership Secrets from the Bible*
New York, NY: MJF Books Fine Communications.

Printed in the United States
by Baker & Taylor Publisher Services